Eyewitness
CASTLE

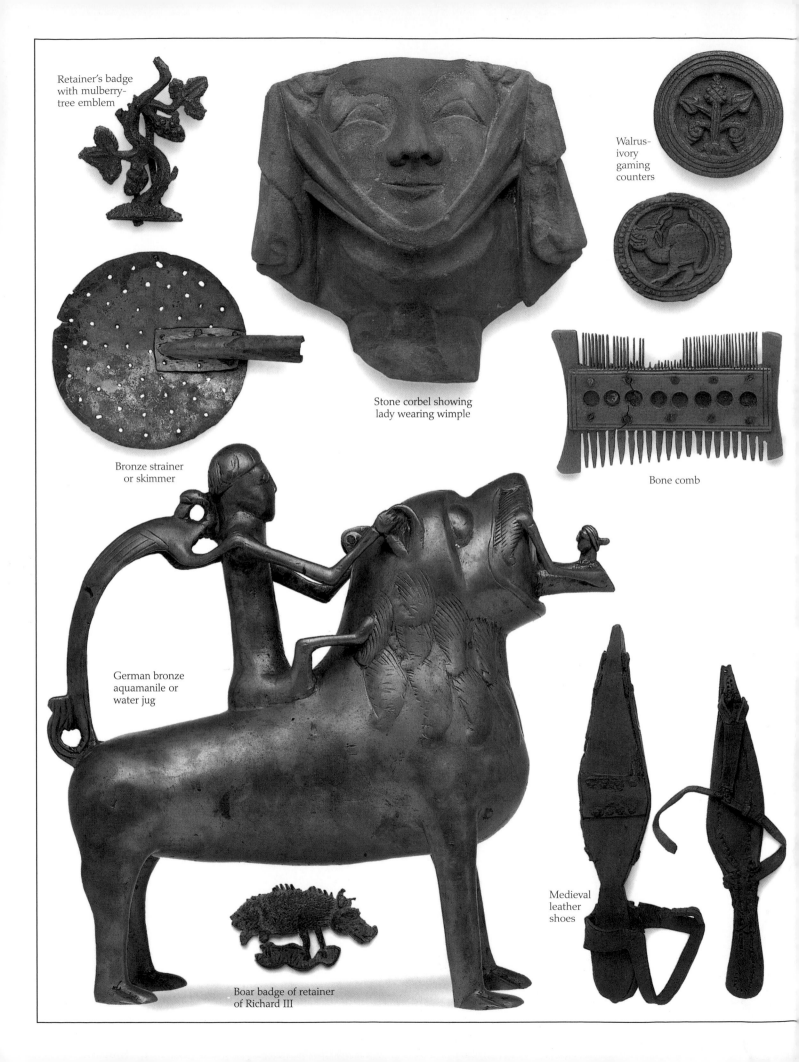

Retainer's badge with mulberry-tree emblem

Stone corbel showing lady wearing wimple

Walrus-ivory gaming counters

Bone comb

Bronze strainer or skimmer

German bronze aquamanile or water jug

Boar badge of retainer of Richard III

Medieval leather shoes

Medieval
musician playing
hornpipe

Eyewitness
CASTLE

Medieval peasant
dressed for work in
the fields

Written by
CHRISTOPHER GRAVETT

Photographed by
GEOFF DANN

Ceramic tiles from Tring, England

English pendant
belonging to
castle retainer

DK Publishing

Italian silver
medallion with arms
of Cresci family

15th-century silver-gilt spoon

Walrus-ivory counter showing burial scene

Late 14th-century table knife

Stone figure of St. George

DK

LONDON, NEW YORK, MELBOURNE, MUNICH, and DELHI

Project editor Phil Wilkinson
Art editor Jane Tetzlaff
Managing editor Simon Adams
Managing art editor Julia Harris
Research Céline Carez
Picture research Kathy Lockley
Production Catherine Semark
Additional Photography
Geoff Brightling, Torla Evans of the Museum of London, Nick Goodall, Allan Hills, Janet Murray of the British Museum, Tim Ridley, and Dave Rudkin

THIS EDITION
Editors Lorrie Mack, Sue Nicholson, Victoria Heywood-Dunne, Marianne Petrou
Art editors Rebecca Johns, David Ball
Managing editors Andrew Macintyre, Camilla Hallinan
Managing art editors Jane Thomas, Martin Wilson
Production editors Siu Yin Ho, Andy Hilliard
Production controllers Jenny Jacoby, Pip Tinsley
Dk picture library Sean Hunter, Rose Horridge, Myriam Megharbi, Emma Shepherd
U.S. editorial Beth Hester, Beth Sutinis
U.S. design & DTP Dirk Kaufman, Milos Orlovic
U.S. production Chris Avgherinos

This Eyewitness ® Guide has been conceived by Dorling Kindersley Limited and Editions Gallimard

This edition published in the United States in 2004, 2008 by DK Publishing, Inc., 375 Hudson Street, New York, New York 10014

Copyright © 1994, 2004, 2008 Dorling Kindersley Limited

12 13 12 11 10 9 8 7
014 – ED634 – Apr/2008

A catalog record for this book is available from the Library of Congress.

ISBN 978-0-7566-3769-9 (HC)
978-0-7566-0659-6 (Library Binding)

Color reproduction by Colourscan, Singapore
Printed and bound in China by South China Printing Co. Ltd

Early 14th-century silver-gilt belt mount

12th-century candlestick from northern Germany

Discover more at

www.dk.com

Earthenware ram's-head jug

Contents

Flemish 15th-century covered wooden bowl (or *mazer*)

What is a castle?

MANY OF THE GREAT fortifications of the Middle Ages are still standing today, often dominating the surrounding countryside. Why were they originally built and who lived in them? A castle was the fortified private residence of a lord. The lord could be a king or a lesser baron, but in either case the castle was a home as well as a stronghold. A mark of lordship, it was safe against the cavalry charge of knights—so safe that it could withstand a continuous assault or siege by an enemy. A castle was also a community, with many staff: the constable or castellan looked after the buildings and defenses; the marshal was in charge of the horses, garrison, and outside servants; the chamberlain oversaw food and drink; and the steward ran the estates and finances.

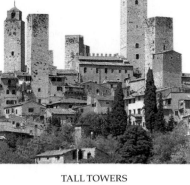

TALL TOWERS
San Gimignano, Italy, is an extreme example of what happened when rival families clashed. Here 72 tall castles were built in the same town, of which 14 survive today.

OLD AND NEW
Castle walls or buildings were often replaced, to make repairs or to build in new defensive features. At Falaise, France, the castle was given a square tower by Henry I in the 12th century and a round one by King Philip Augustus in the early 13th century.

ANCESTOR
At Mycenae, Greece, a strong fortified-palace was built in about 1250 BCE. The Lion Gate guards the entrance. Such a state-run building is not a true castle, even though it has large stone fortifications.

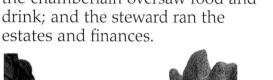

IRON AGE
The large earthworks at Maiden Castle, England, are actually the remains of a Celtic palisaded settlement built on a New Stone Age site. It was thus more like a fortified town than a castle. It was captured by the Romans.

Natural rocky outcrop provides base for castle

MASTER
This early 14th-century picture shows a king instructing a master mason, who was in charge of the castle's construction. He carries a set square. Some kings built numerous castles but only lived in them occasionally.

Main stone tower on top of mound

Inner curtain wall

SYMBOL OF POWER
As well as being a home, the castle was a symbol of power. Caernarfon in north Wales, begun together with a walled town in 1283, was one of a series of castles built by Edward I of England in order to overawe the people of Wales.

TURKISH TOWERS
Van Castle in Turkey was begun in 850 CE. During the Middle Ages it was repaired by the Seljuk and Ottoman Turks, and was later lived in by Armenian Christians.

Steep crag makes castle difficult to attack

MEETING PLACE
Castles were often the scenes of important meetings about state affairs. This picture shows the meeting of Richard II and his uncle the Duke of Gloucester that took place at Pleshey Castle.

The first castles

THE EARLIEST CASTLES appeared in the 9th and 10th centuries, when the empire created by Charlemagne in modern France, Germany, and North Italy was collapsing as a result of raids by peoples such as Vikings and Magyars. Lords built castles for protection and as bases for their soldiers. Most of these castles were built of earth and timber. The simplest was the ringwork: an enclosure surrounded by a ditch with an earth rampart inside it. A strong timber fence (or palisade) was built on top of the rampart. In the 11th century, motte and bailey castles became popular. An earth mound (or motte) was built next to a yard (or bailey).

CEASTRA

BUILDING A MOTTE
The Bayeux Tapestry, probably made between 1066 and 1086, shows a motte being built at Hastings, England, by the Normans. The motte is being made of rammed layers of soil, although no evidence of this method has been found in the real motte at Hastings.

LAST REMAINS
A motte with two baileys was built at Yelden, England, probably soon after the Norman conquest. The ditches were fed by a local stream. Often a grassy mound like this is all that remains of an early castle.

Lifting bridge

Timber palisade

Stables

Thatched roof

Hall

Courtyard or bailey

Castle yard
or bailey

Earth
motte

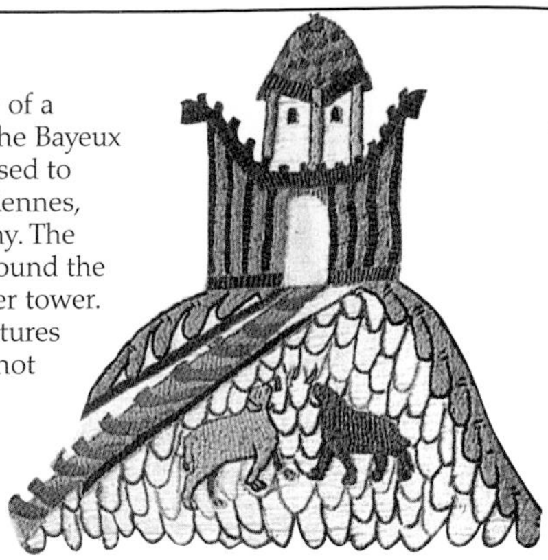

TIMBER TOWER
This stylized picture of a
motte comes from the Bayeux
Tapestry. It is supposed to
show the castle at Rennes,
the capital of Brittany. The
wooden palisade around the
top encloses a timber tower.
If it were not for pictures
like this, we would not
know what these
towers looked like.

PLESHEY
The large motte and bailey at Pleshey, England, was built
by the Normans soon after 1066. This type of castle could
be erected in a matter of months rather than years, which
was ideal when the Normans were in a hostile country.
Pleshey castle has one motte and one bailey, but sometimes
there were two mottes or two baileys.

Roof of
wooden
shingles

Wooden
stilts to give
space under
tower

MOTTE AND BAILEY
These castles were increasingly built in the 11th and 12th
centuries. There was a courtyard, or bailey, protected by a
ditch and palisade and with an entrance gate often with a
lifting bridge, a drawbridge, or even a timber gate tower.
Within the bailey were stables and workshops, a well, and
perhaps a chapel. The motte was the final refuge. Many
mottes were only about 15 ft (5 m) high, but some were
twice that size. The tower on top was usually of wood—
stone ones were often too heavy for artificial mounds.
Some towers had many rooms, but if there was
only space for a watchtower on the motte, a
great hall might be built in the bailey.

Timber
walkway

Earth mound
or motte

Timber flying
bridge

The great tower

During the tenth century, lords began to build castles out of stone. A large stone tower could become the main military and residential building of a castle. Because they needed skilled masons to plan and build them, and were expensive and slow to put up, few such towers were built until the 11th century. They are now often known as keeps, but in their day they were called great towers, or donjons. The Normans liked great towers with massively thick stone walls, and built several after their conquest of England in 1066. Many more were built in the next century. They were stronger than walls of wood and did not burn. Attackers had to use other ways to destroy them, such as chipping away at the corners with picks, or digging tunnels beneath (undermining) the foundations to weaken them. Later round or many-sided towers had no sharp angles and gave defenders a better field of fire.

PRISON
Great towers had many different uses. Here the Duke of Orleans, captured by the English at the Battle of Agincourt in 1415, awaits his ransom. He is held in the White Tower, in the middle of the Tower of London.

HOARDINGS
The octagonal tower at Provins, France, built in about 1150, is shown here with wooden hoardings (pp.28–29) that were added later.

SHELL
As stone defenses became more common, the wooden palisades around the top of a motte (pp.8–9) were sometimes replaced with stone walls for added strength. Structures like this are now called shell keeps. This shell keep is at Restormel, Cornwall. It has strong stone walls and a roomy courtyard within the walls.

Double windows provide more light

KEEPING WARM
In wooden buildings the fire was made in an open hearth in the middle of the floor. But with a stone tower, fireplaces could be built into the thickness of the wall. The flue passed through the wall to the outside and carried much of the smoke away from the room.

Zigzag decoration, typical of buildings of the 12th century

GREAT HALL
One floor of the great tower of Hedingham Castle was used as the great hall, in which the lord and his household lived and ate. To light the hall, large alcoves were set into the thickness of the walls. Doors in some of the alcoves lead to lavatories or rooms (mural chambers) set into the walls. The level above has a mural gallery, set within the wall, which runs all the way around the hall.

Window in alcove

ROUND HEAD
The windows at Hedingham have round arches typical of the style called Romanesque or Norman.

Narrow opening to stop the entry of arrows

MANY-SIDED TOWER
The 12th-century castle at Orford, England, is polygonal. Instead of four sharp corners, the builders experimented with shallower angles. These, together with round towers, helped guard against undermining.

Flag of castle owner

Stair turret, also used as a watchtower

Finely cut facing stone (ashlar)

HEDINGHAM CASTLE
The great tower at Hedingham, England, was built by Aubrey de Vere in around 1142 to celebrate his being made an earl, perhaps as a showpiece for entertaining guests. It is not a large keep but still has the interior strengthened by an arch on the first and second floors.

Wall walk (now lacking battlements)

Decorative false windows to make tower look more imposing

Gallery of the great hall

Great hall

Brick and rubble infill

Door to entrance floor

Surviving lower portion of stone forebuilding

Concentric castles

By THE MID-13TH CENTURY some castles were built with rings of stone walls one inside the other. These are called concentric castles. The outer wall was fairly close to and lower than the inner, sometimes so low that it seemed no more than a barrier against siege engines. But it meant that archers on the inner walls could shoot over the heads of those on the outer, bringing twice the firepower to bear on an enemy. If attackers broke through the outer wall, they would still be faced with the inner wall. Sometimes towers could be sealed off, leaving the enemy exposed on the wall-walks of the outer wall. In older castles the great tower and curtain wall were sometimes given an outer ring of walls, making three separate lines of defense.

GATEHOUSE
This is the gatehouse on a dam wall that leads to the outer eastern gate at Caerphilly Castle. The twin holes above the archway are for the chains of a lifting bridge. Behind this were a portcullis and double doors. Notice the "spurs" that jut out to strengthen the base of each tower.

Holes to
take timber
supports for
hoardings

Gatehouse

Round
corner
tower

Outer
curtain
wall

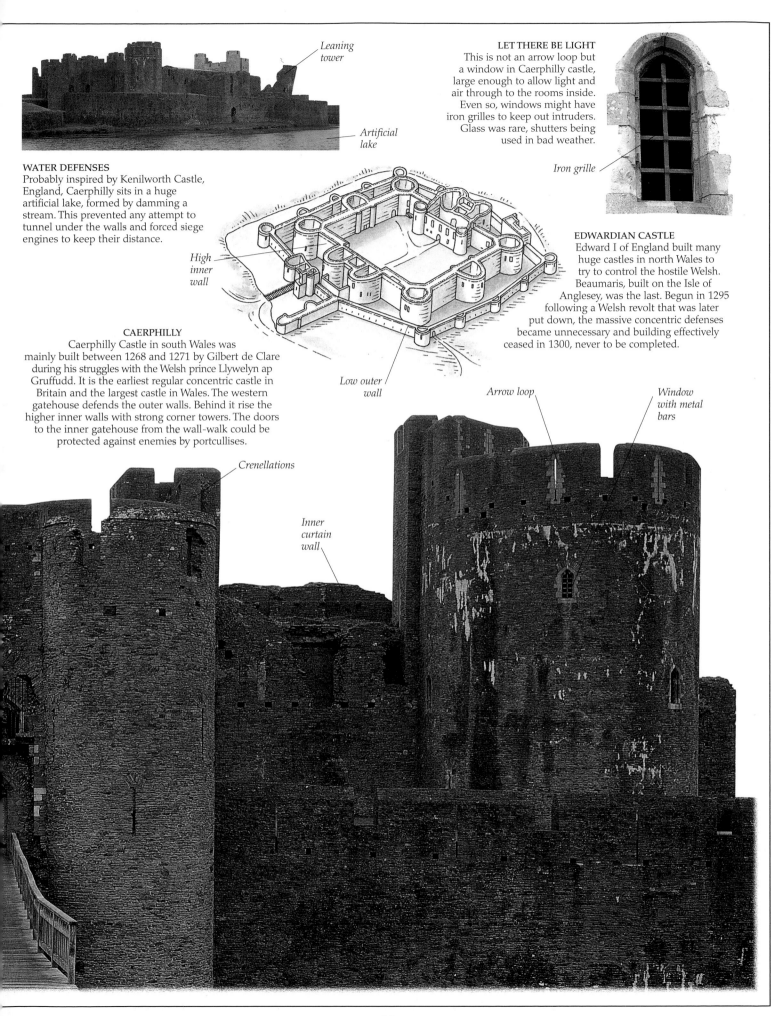

Leaning tower

Artificial lake

WATER DEFENSES

Probably inspired by Kenilworth Castle, England, Caerphilly sits in a huge artificial lake, formed by damming a stream. This prevented any attempt to tunnel under the walls and forced siege engines to keep their distance.

High inner wall

LET THERE BE LIGHT

This is not an arrow loop but a window in Caerphilly castle, large enough to allow light and air through to the rooms inside. Even so, windows might have iron grilles to keep out intruders. Glass was rare, shutters being used in bad weather.

Iron grille

EDWARDIAN CASTLE

Edward I of England built many huge castles in north Wales to try to control the hostile Welsh. Beaumaris, built on the Isle of Anglesey, was the last. Begun in 1295 following a Welsh revolt that was later put down, the massive concentric defenses became unnecessary and building effectively ceased in 1300, never to be completed.

CAERPHILLY

Caerphilly Castle in south Wales was mainly built between 1268 and 1271 by Gilbert de Clare during his struggles with the Welsh prince Llywelyn ap Gruffudd. It is the earliest regular concentric castle in Britain and the largest castle in Wales. The western gatehouse defends the outer walls. Behind it rise the higher inner walls with strong corner towers. The doors to the inner gatehouse from the wall-walk could be protected against enemies by portcullises.

Low outer wall

Arrow loop

Window with metal bars

Crenellations

Inner curtain wall

13

Castles on the Loire

MANY CASTLES were built along the Loire River in France. Doué-la-Fontaine, probably the oldest known keep, was one of the first. French castles developed during the reign of Philip Augustus (1180–1223) with powerful keeps, enclosures, round towers, and towers *en bec* (like a beak) on which the outward-facing side is drawn out like a ship's prow. Flying turrets jutted from walls without reaching the ground, and towers often had tall, conical roofs. In the 15th century, French castles became more luxurious.

Polychrome jug

Floor tiles

FRENCH TASTES
The 14th century polychrome (many-colored) jug is in typical French style. The floor tiles are from Saumur Castle and bear heraldic pictures. The fleur-de-lis was used in French royal arms and became the symbol of the French royal house. It therefore appeared in the coats-of-arms of a number of related families.

Rope for hauling bucket

Wooden teeth

Wooden cog wheel

Strong wooden framework

Crank handle

WINDER
At Saumur, water could be brought up from an underground well using these winding wheels. The wheels are made of wood and the teeth of one mesh with holes in the other.

ENTRANCE
Stone steps now lead up to the entrance at Saumur, which is flanked on either side by flying turrets. Materials could be dropped from above the gate on enemies attacking the castle. On the right, a concave ramp allows goods to be dragged or barrels rolled up or down it.

SAUMUR *right*
Saumur Castle may have been begun as early as the 10th century but has been rebuilt several times. By the 15th century it had a fairy-tale appearance, complete with golden weathercocks, as shown in a picture from the Duke of Berry's book, *Très riches heures*. It became a comfortable residence but was abandoned in the 17th century when the west wing fell down. It was then used as a prison and barracks, but was later restored.

LORDS AND LADIES
French nobles always felt themselves to be among the leaders of fashion and French courts were centers of elegance. These lords and ladies of the turn of the 16th century are dressed in expensive robes.

THE VINEYARDS

The illustration of September from the Duke of Berry's *Très riches heures* of about 1416 shows the grape harvest in the vineyard below the whitewashed walls of Saumur Castle. The lower windows have iron grilles to stop people from getting in. The upper parts, although machicolated, have fantastic Gothic-style carved traceries. The barbican gate has both a small and a large lifting bridge. On its left are small jutting latrine blocks that drop waste into ditches. To their left is the tall chimney of the kitchen, isolated to guard against spreading fire.

Stair tower

Well house

WELL

The courtyard at Saumur has a well with a large underground water tank. This tank extends under the covered well house on the left, which contains the winding mechanism for lifting large buckets.

Corner tower

Stair turret with conical roof

Machicolations

Castles in Spain

SPAIN HAD MUSLIM rulers (Moors) from 711 CE until the Christians took their last stronghold, Granada, in 1492. The Muslims used a different style from the Christians—for example, building square or wedge-shaped towered *alcazabas* (garrison forts). Their enemies, the Christian knights, built *torres del homenaje* (tower-keeps) that were often round. From the 14th century on, the Christians pushed south; they built castles more like those found in England and France. Later still, conflicts between king and nobles led to a style of fortress that mixed Moorish and Christian styles.

SHIP OF STONE
The *Alcázar* (palace) of Segovia, rebuilt in the early 15th century, is called a *gran buque* or "great ship" castle because of its long shape. The earlier keep was separated from the new tower-keep.

Decorative false machicolations mimic the real thing but have no gaps for dropping missiles

Ball decoration

Crenellated corner tower

Coat-of-arms

Arrow slit

A SIEGE
The wall-towers are packed with soldiers in this 13th-century Spanish wall fresco of the attack on Mallorca. On the right, a staff sling is about to be released. This was a sling attached to a wooden pole that extended the range its stone or lead missile could be hurled.

Octagonal turret

CASTLE PALACE
Heavily influenced by Moorish styles, el Real de Manzanares, north of Madrid, was built in 1475 for the first duke of the Infantado. It is almost square and is surrounded by two sets of walls with round towers. In 1480, the second duke added the gallery, turret, and ball decoration.

ALL A GAME
The Moors lived in Spain after they conquered it in the 8th century. They established a civilization there that in many ways was well in advance of Christian Europe. From the 10th century, Christians, including religious orders of monk-knights, tried to seize Spain from them. Here two Moors play a form of chess.

GRANADA
In 1492 the town of Granada in southern Spain, the last Moorish stronghold in Spain, fell to the Christians. The Alhambra is a fortified palace set on a nearby hill and is full of beautiful Moorish decorations, like these graceful arches around a courtyard.

Ornate gallery

Inner curtain wall

Outer curtain wall

Castles in Germany

IN WHAT IS NOW GERMANY, many princes and nobles lived in castles under the leadership of an emperor. As central control broke down in the 13th century, many lesser lords also built castles, some as bases for robbery. German castle design was often influenced by the landscape. Many castles took advantage of the hills and mountains. Others were built along the banks of the Rhine. In flatter areas, the *Wasserburg*, a castle protected by a wide moat, was built. The Teutonic Order of monk knights built brick castles like blockhouses, containing residential and religious areas set around a rectangular courtyard. Most large 11th- and 12th-century castles were later given a surrounding wall with flanking towers.

POTTERY
This type of pottery is known as Rhenish ware because it was made in the Rhineland. It was often exported to other countries. These jugs would have been "thrown" on a potter's wheel and partly glazed to add color.

LONG OCCUPATION
Schloss Mespelbrunn at Spessart, Bavaria, began as a medieval castle and was rebuilt in the 16th century to suit the taste for more comfort. Because the castle sits in a huge moat, its builders could put large windows in the outer walls.

HILLTOP HOME
Cochem Castle sits on a hill overlooking the Moselle River. It was probably begun in about 1020. The tall tower or *Bergfried* is typically German. The castle was used as a toll station, and there was a chain to bar the river.

Handle

spout

Hollow body for water

LION JUG
The aquamanile was a type of metal or pottery jug filled at the top and with a spout to pour water for washing hands at mealtimes. Different forms were made, including jugs in the shape of knights on horseback. This German copper-alloy lion has a man sitting astride its back, pulling its ears.

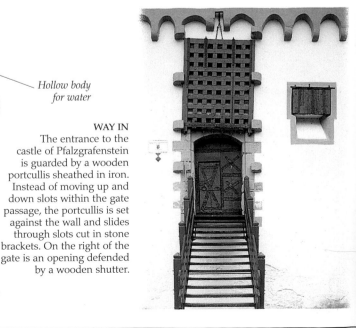

WAY IN
The entrance to the castle of Pfalzgrafenstein is guarded by a wooden portcullis sheathed in iron. Instead of moving up and down slots within the gate passage, the portcullis is set against the wall and slides through slots cut in stone brackets. On the right of the gate is an opening defended by a wooden shutter.

ISLAND CASTLE
The five-sided tower of the Pfalzgrafenstein
was built as a toll station on an island in the
Rhine by King Ludwig I of Bavaria in 1327.

THE ENCLOSURE
This view from the tower of
the Pfalzgrafenstein shows
the domestic buildings set
against the inner side of the
enclosure walls. A covered
wooden gallery runs
alongside these buildings.
In the middle is one of the
circular turrets that
cover the angles where
two walls meet.

*Belfry on
medieval
tower*

HOME COMFORTS
The latrine or privy
has a wooden seat to
give added
comfort.

Gun ports

A CASTLE REUSED
The hexagonal enclosure of the
Pfalzgrafenstein was added
between about 1338 and 1342
to create a turret fortress,
a type of castle typical of
western Germany. Useful
even after the end of
the Middle Ages, it was
strengthened further
in 1607, when one
end was given a
protruding bastion.

Window

*Wooden
hoarding
for defense*

*Seventeenth-
century bastion*

Continued on next page

LOOK TO HEAVEN
The painted ceiling of the chapel in the Marksburg gives some idea of the type of interior decoration used. Like many German castles, this one had small, homey rooms rather than great halls.

FLOOR TILE
This tile came from the Marksburg. It shows how lords tried to brighten up what must have been rather cold and uncomfortable rooms.

GROWING CASTLE
The central tower of the Marksburg, near the Rhine in Germany, dates from the early Middle Ages and has gradually been surrounded by later defenses. It has small flying turrets in French style, but the arched friezes rising above the walls are typical of the Rhineland.

Castles on crags

In some areas, especially in Germany, castle-builders took advantage of hilly or mountainous countryside. The steepness made assault by men or siege engines difficult, and rock foundations deterred mining. When central control broke down in Germany in the mid-13th century and many of the lesser German barons built castles, they found that one of the cheapest ways was to circle the top of a crag with a wall. This was often rebuilt with flanking towers as these became common in the rest of Europe. A deep ditch was dug on the weakest side, or a very high mantle wall erected. If all sides needed equal protection, the walls might surround a central tower. Otherwise the domestic buildings were fortified and set around the courtyard to form a type of castle called a *Randhausburg*.

Glazed earthenware cooking pot

Barred door

Metal skimmer

Flue rises through thickness of castle wall

Flat-bottomed iron pot

Ladle

WALL SPACE
This niche in the wall has been given a shelf and filled with jugs behind a barred door.

BUILDING WORK
This German illustration portrays the Biblical story of the Tower of Babel. Although the tower was supposed to have been built long before the Medieval period, the workers are using the methods that German builders would have used to construct a castle.

WELCOME GLOW
Food was cooked over the kitchen fire in medieval castles (see pp.40–41). This kitchen fireplace in the Pfalzgrafenstein has a metal cooking pot hanging over the fire. Pots and bowls stand ready on the shelf above and a metal ladle and a skimmer hang to one side. Because kitchens had fires, there was always a possible danger. Sometimes the kitchen was put in a separate building, and sometimes it was separated from the great hall by a passage, which gave some added safety.

FACT OR FICTION?
This gun-toting cavalryman appears in a German military design manual of the early 15th century. The gun is attached to his chest and steadied by a rod fixed to the saddle. It is not known whether the design was ever used.

Circular main tower

Machicolations

Wooden belfry

Decorative finial

Stepped gable

LICHTENSTEIN
This castle in Wurttemberg was begun in the early 13th century and is divided into a northern and a southern part. This layout is the result of the castle's being occupied by several members of a family at once. This type of fortification is sometimes seen in Germany. Both parts have a square or rectangular watchtower. The northern section also has a round tower and a Romanesque chapel; the southern part has half-timbered frontages on to a courtyard.

CHANGING NEEDS
It is said that this window was filled in during the Thirty Years War in the 17th century, leaving a staggered arrow loop to be used in times of trouble.

Hall with large windows

Gatehouse with wooden drawbridge

The chapel

The dead were wrapped in cloth shrouds. A coffin was often used to take a dead body to the grave.

THE CHAPEL WAS an important room in a Christian castle, because inhabitants were expected to attend regular services. In early towers the chapel was often on the top floor or in an upper room in the entrance building. As castles developed, the chapel became part of the domestic range of buildings. It might be decorated with carved stonework and wall paintings that often illustrated a Bible story, because few people could read the Bible itself and so many relied on pictures. The clergy were among the few who could read and write and so, in addition to their religious duties, they looked after the documents relating to the castle. A chaplain therefore often had several clerks to help him.

FAITH AND POLITICS
This 15th-century illustration shows Thomas Arundel, archbishop of Canterbury, England, preaching the cause of Henry IV. Banished by Richard II, Henry IV landed in England in 1399 with Thomas and, supported by a group of nobles, seized the crown. Medieval churchmen were often mixed up with political intrigues. Bishops did not work in castle chapels; the most powerful of them held castles in their own right.

ROYAL CUP
The Royal Gold Cup was made in about 1380 for the Duke of Berry in France and has been in the possession of both English and French kings. It is decorated in colored enamels with scenes of saints' lives—religious teaching was always present in every medieval household.

Scene of the Adoration of the Magi

Magi awakened by an angel

TEACHING IN STONE
The entrance to the chapel at the castle of Loches in France dates from the late 12th century. The doorway is carved with figures that were designed to help teach people who were unable to read.

Statue of a bishop

Carvings of animals and mythical beasts

Saint Peter

Holy water stoup

This miter (bishop's hat) was probably Becket's

SEAL
Becket's seal shows an early miter worn side-on. Later bishops, like Thomas Arundel on the opposite page, wore their miters front-on, as bishops do today.

Sword with broad, diamond-sectioned blade

Gauntlet

Priest attending Becket

Thomas Becket in prayer at the altar

Poleyn

MARTYRDOM
This piece of alabaster is carved with a scene of the death of Thomas Becket in 1170, though the knights all wear armor of the late 14th century, when the carving was made. Becket was archbishop of Canterbury under Henry II of England, but the two men constantly argued. After an angry outburst by Henry, four knights murdered Becket in his own cathedral. He was soon hailed as a saint and Canterbury became a great shrine for pilgrims.

Laying a siege

IF SURROUNDING a castle and trying to starve the defenders into submission did not work, attackers could try to take it by force. They could tunnel under the walls to bring them down, or come up inside the courtyard. Defenders might place bowls of water on the ground so that any tunneling activity made the water ripple. Then they could dig countermines to break into the tunnels, leading to a fierce struggle underground. They could also try to break down the walls using artillery or battering rams slung under movable sheds. Defenders lowered hooks to catch the heads of battering rams, or dropped mattresses to cushion the blows. A direct assault over the walls meant using scaling ladders to hook on to battlements; this was dangerous, as defenders pushed them away with forked poles.

CHIPPING AWAY
Under cover of a shed on wheels, miners pick away stones at the wall base. Inserted wood props were then burned to make the wall collapse. Raw or wet hides protected the wood from fire.

Wheel to move shield

MOVABLE SHIELD
Archers and crossbowmen used these shields to protect themselves while trying to pick off defenders and covering assaults.

PEOPLE POWER
The traction trebuchet, which probably appeared in the mid-12th century, had a team of men hauling on ropes at the short end of a beam, pivoting up the other end with its sling. This opened to release a large stone.

Ropes for hauling

Sling

Pivoting arm

MOUTHPIECE
From the 12th century, heralds were used to demand surrender on their lord's behalf. They wore the lord's coat-of-arms for recognition.

Counterweight

Large stones for use as missiles

HEAVYWEIGHT
The counterpoise trebuchet, which probably appeared in the late 12th century, used a huge box of soil and stones instead of manpower to pull down the arm and send a missile flying into the air.

Winch

KEEP YOUR HEAD UP
Severed enemy heads were sometimes thrown to demoralize the opposition. Messengers with rejected terms might be trussed up in a trebuchet, or dung or dead animals thrown to spread disease.

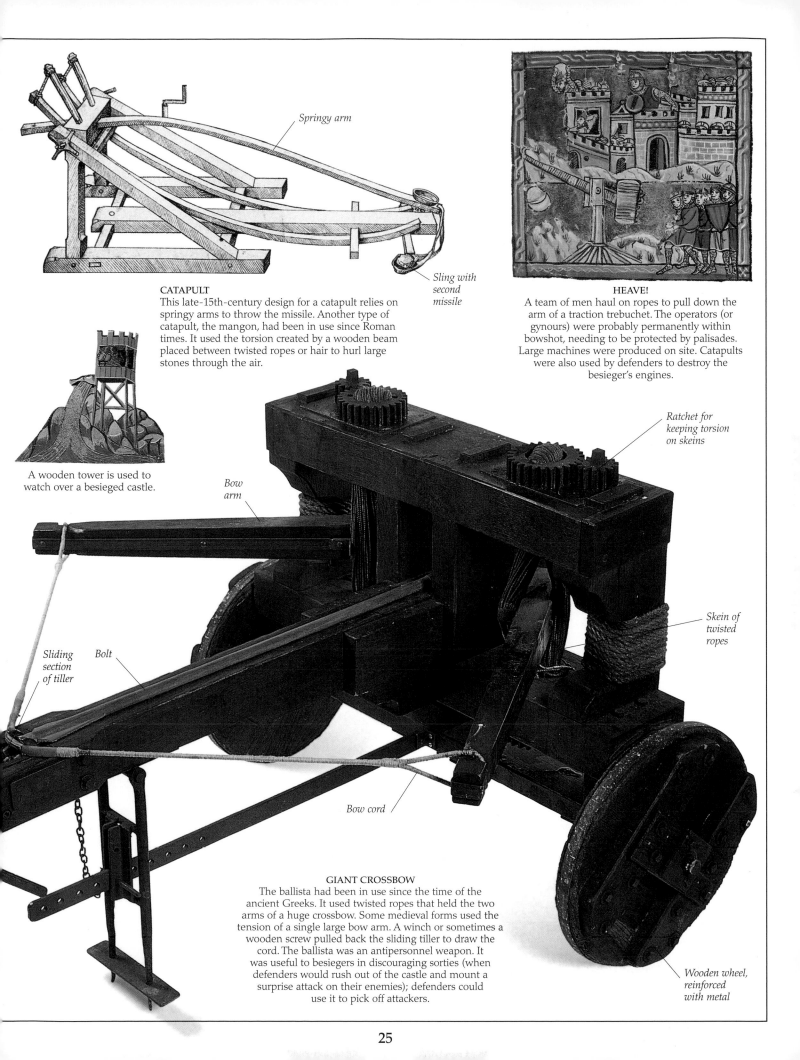

CATAPULT
This late-15th-century design for a catapult relies on springy arms to throw the missile. Another type of catapult, the mangon, had been in use since Roman times. It used the torsion created by a wooden beam placed between twisted ropes or hair to hurl large stones through the air.

Springy arm

Sling with second missile

A wooden tower is used to watch over a besieged castle.

HEAVE!
A team of men haul on ropes to pull down the arm of a traction trebuchet. The operators (or gynours) were probably permanently within bowshot, needing to be protected by palisades. Large machines were produced on site. Catapults were also used by defenders to destroy the besieger's engines.

Ratchet for keeping torsion on skeins

Bow arm

Skein of twisted ropes

Sliding section of tiller

Bolt

Bow cord

GIANT CROSSBOW
The ballista had been in use since the time of the ancient Greeks. It used twisted ropes that held the two arms of a huge crossbow. Some medieval forms used the tension of a single large bow arm. A winch or sometimes a wooden screw pulled back the sliding tiller to draw the cord. The ballista was an antipersonnel weapon. It was useful to besiegers in discouraging sorties (when defenders would rush out of the castle and mount a surprise attack on their enemies); defenders could use it to pick off attackers.

Wooden wheel, reinforced with metal

Men and missiles

CASTLES HAD SPECIAL features to protect the defenders while allowing them to shoot at their enemies. Battlements and loopholes enabled archers to cover a wide area in front of the castle. The gaps (or crenels) in the battlements were sometimes fitted with shutters to deflect missiles. The stone parts of the battlements (the merlons) might also have loopholes for archers to shoot through. To guard against missiles, surprise attacks (sorties) by the garrison, and assault by relief forces, besiegers might surround their lines with palisades. Sometimes they moved on but left a timber "siege castle" full of men to watch the castle.

OVER THE WATER
Some castles had a wet moat or lake and others were actually built near a river or the seashore. Occasionally attackers brought up boats that contained scaling ladders or even wooden towers from which they tried to cross the walls.

NARROW LOOPHOLES
These holes were usually splayed on the inside to form an embrasure or open chamber within the wall. The archer probably stood just to one side of this, looking through the hole until an enemy came within range. Then he would move to the center of the embrasure to shoot. Enemy marksmen may have shot arrows through loopholes, especially if shooting at close range.

Crank handle

Pulley

Windlass cord

WINDLASS
Some crossbows were so powerful that a windlass was needed to draw back the thick cord attached to the bow-arm. Turning the handles wound up the windlass cords, which were attached by hooks to the cord of the bow. Pulleys reduced the effort needed to pull the cord.

Crossbow cord

Bow arm

ARROWS
The longbow came to prominence in the 12th century. It could send its arrows at least 1,000 ft (300 m). A longbowman could shoot about 12 arrows in the time it took to load a crossbow, but the strength needed to pull the bow meant that they needed regular practice.

Wooden shaft   *Feather fletching*

Leather flight

Knock to take bow string

Stirrup

QUARREL
Crossbows shot short arrows called bolts. Because of their four-sided heads, they were also known as quarrels, from *carre*, the old French word for four.

Wooden shaft

Iron point

Cord drawn back

Bow arm

Tiller

Stirrup

Bolt

The bolts were carried in a quiver slung from the waist; in a castle they could be supplied from barrels

THE CROSSBOW
Crossbows were powerful but slow to reload. For this reason their use in a castle was ideal, because the crossbowman could prepare his weapon from behind the safety of the walls. In some cases a second crossbow might be loaded by an assistant while the crossbowman was aiming the first one, speeding up the process.

GOING UP
Spiral staircases were common in medieval castles. Each stair ended in a circular slab and the next stair was laid with this end over the one below, so creating the cylindrical newel post. Such stairs often spiral up in a clockwise direction; this may have been deliberately done to hamper an attacker fighting his way up the stairs, whose weapon (in his right hand) would keep hitting the stonework.

SHIELDED
Besieging crossbowmen also needed protection when reloading.

SURRENDER
The burghers of Calais surrender to the English king Edward III in 1340. The victor received the keys of the stronghold. Defenders who refused to surrender immediately faced looting, pillage, and death if they were defeated.

Tricks of defense

THE FIRST OBSTACLE faced by someone attacking a castle was a wet or dry moat. A moat made it difficult for attackers to bring siege engines close to the castle. In a dry moat, stakes might be planted to slow an enemy and make him an easier target. The gatehouse was an obvious weak spot, so a defensive work or *barbican* was sometimes placed in front to guard the approach. A drawbridge and portcullises gave extra protection. The portcullis was made of iron or an iron-covered wooden grille that moved up and down in slots on either side of the entrance passage. It was raised by a winch in a room above and could be dropped quickly if danger threatened. Drawbridges over the ditch took several forms, including simple wooden platforms that were pulled back, lifting bridges attached by chains to pulleys, and turning bridges pivoted like a seesaw.

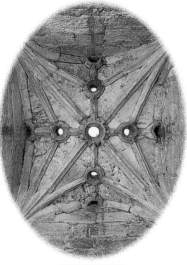

DROPPING IN
The gate passage at Bodiam has so-called "murder holes" (*meutrières*) in the roof so cold water could be poured down to put out fires. Scalding water, hot sand, or other offensive substances might be also dropped on enemies who managed to get in.

GATEHOUSE
In this example, the passage is flanked by huge towers. Missiles could be dropped on an attacker through slots over the arch.

FLARING BASE
The Castel Nuovo (New Castle) in Naples, Italy, has a small outer wall or *chemise*. This wall has a splayed-out base (called a batter or talus), so that missiles dropped from above would bounce out toward the enemy. It also thickened the wall, giving added protection against attacks by battering rams, undermining, or bombardment. The castle was rebuilt in the years 1442–58 as an early experiment against artillery, so this example was also designed to deflect enemy cannon balls.

Curtain wall

Corbel

Batter or talus

MACHICOLATIONS
Machicolations were stone versions of wooden hoardings and appeared in the 12th century. The battlements jutted beyond the walls and were supported on stone corbels. Gaps left between the corbels allowed offensive material to be dropped on enemies at the wall base.

GUN PORT
In the late 14th century, keyhole-shaped gun ports appeared. Round ports were usually for handguns, while horizontal slots were for small cannon mounted behind walls. This example is from the Pfalzgrafenstein in Germany.

STICKING OUT
The Pfalzgrafenstein on the Rhine has a number of hoardings built out from the tops of its walls. These are wooden constructions with gaps in the floor allowing defenders to drop missiles on attackers at the foot of the wall without having to expose themselves by leaning out over the battlements. Hot water, red-hot sand, or rocks might be thrown, as well as quicklime. Boiling oil, beloved of film-makers, is rarely mentioned.

Steep roof to throw off missiles

Slots for observation and shooting through

Wooden walls

Timber support

LIFTING BRIDGES
The *bascule* bridge had chains attached to wooden beams weighted at the rear. This end dropped when released, lifting the front of the bridge into recesses in the wall.

Manuscript showing lifting bridge with wooden beams and chains

Pedestrian and main lifting bridges at Langeais, France

Machicolated parapet

Turret for observation

Round tower less vulnerable to miners than sharp angles

Portcullis

Gun port

CURTAINS AND FLANKS
The 14th-century castle at Bodiam, England, has stretches of curtain walls protected by flanking towers which jut out beyond the wall face.

The garrison

Basinet

Mail curtain (or aventail)

THE BODY OF SOLDIERS who lived in a castle and defended it was called the garrison. In early castles, especially at times of unrest, these men might be knights who lived permanently in their lord's castle. In return for accommodation, they fought for the lord and guarded the castle. Gradually more knights settled on their own estates and the duty was performed using a rota system. A knight stayed in the castle for a set period, then he was replaced by another man. In the 14th and 15th centuries it was common for hired soldiers to be used to guard castles. It was once thought that the lord's rooms were sometimes built over the gate because of fear of betrayal.

Part of shield

Steel gauntlet

Jupon

UNDER SIEGE
The garrison was vital in times of siege. In this German manuscript of the early 14th century, the women of the castle help out the hard-pressed defenders.

HORSE DECOR
In the 14th and 15th centuries the bridle and breast straps of horses were often decorated with enameled pendants made of copper alloy. This one bears the arms of the Berkeley family.

MAN OF STEEL
By the later 14th century, as shown by this stone figure of St. George, a knight's limbs were often enclosed in steel plates and a coat-of-plates was worn under a tight quilted or cloth garment called a jupon. The steel helmet, called a basinet, is fitted with a curtain of mail to protect the sides of the head and neck. This figure carries a shield, although these were becoming less common by this time.

KNIGHTLY DUTIES
Castles usually had only a small garrison in peacetime, and even in
times of trouble, soldiers were counted in tens rather than in hundreds.
The garrison provided a ready supply of knights, men-at-arms, and
squires when a lord needed them. Armed men were not only needed
in wartime; lords used them for escort duties, to protect them
on the roads, especially from robbers in wooded areas. In this
14th-century picture, the arrival of mailed men is greeted
by fanfares from the castle.

Loop for chain

Dragon emblem

*Round-topped
shield, typically
Italian in shape*

*Arms of
Cresci
family*

DRAGON
This badge
dates from the
15th century and
depicts a dragon.
This creature was a
common emblem in
heraldry. The badge is
decorated with enamel,
and was worn as a pendant.

*Worn white
enamel
decoration*

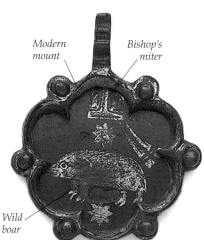

*Modern
mount*

*Bishop's
miter*

*Wild
boar*

MEDALLION
This silver medallion comes from Florence, Italy,
and dates to the 14th century. The right-hand
shield may show the arms of the Cresci family,
suggesting that it could have belonged to one of
that family's retainers.

OLD BOAR
This 15th-century horse pendant was,
like the others, cast in copper alloy and
decorated with enamel. The decoration
shows a wild boar and a bishop's miter.
The pendant has been cut down
and mounted.

MULBERRY BUSH
This badge of a mulberry bush belonged to a
retainer of the Mowbray family. Followers
of noble families often wore metal
badges like this, or cloth badges
stitched to their clothing for
identification.

FIGHTING MAN
Knights who garrisoned
Norman castles had coats of
mail, steel helmets, and large
wooden shields.

THORN IN THE SIDE
Castles were not just
fortified dwellings. They
were bases from which
soldiers controlled the
surrounding countryside.
This meant that an
invader had to detach
soldiers to take castles,
or run the risk that his
supply lines would be cut.

The castle as prison

A CASTLE SEEMS AN IDEAL PLACE for keeping prisoners. In medieval times most prisoners were political or state prisoners. Some of them were captured noblemen awaiting the payment of ransom money. They were given good living conditions, because they were valueless to their captors if they died. Such men might even give their word of honor not to escape, in return for some freedom. Most rooms called "dungeons" were probably cellars—only the ones with difficult access may have been prisons. These were sometimes called *oubliettes*, a French word suggesting that the prisoners were left and forgotten. Criminals were not imprisoned in castles in the Middle Ages. They were usually punished by fine, mutilation, or execution. More castles were used as prisons after the Middle Ages. In fact, most stories involving torture, imprisonment, and execution taking place in castles belong after the Middle Ages, in the 16th and 17th centuries.

Welsh prince Gruffydd falls to his death trying to escape from the Tower of London in 1244.

MANACLES
This iron collar is attached to a chain, which was in turn secured to the wall of a room in Loches castle. Adding to the discomfort, the collar weighs about 35 lb (16 kg). Few men of rank would be kept in such conditions.

Locking iron ring

Heavy iron chain attached to wall

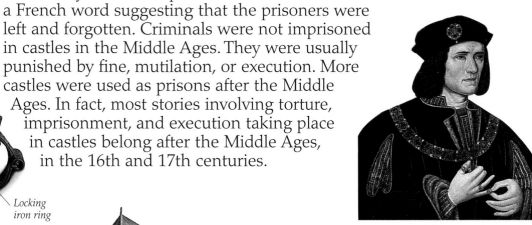

Part of castle containing prison

Barred window

GOOD KING RICHARD?
The English king Richard III was said to have ordered the murder of his two nephews, Edward V and Richard, in the Tower of London in 1483. The princes were kept in the Tower to prevent nobles from using them as rivals for the throne. Nobody knows who really killed them or exactly when they died.

A PRISON
The keep at Loches, France, was used as a prison from the 15th century. This example, together with a few others such as the Tower of London, may imply that blood and death were common in such places. But most stories of prisoners' misery belong in later times, when castles were used for political executions or as common jails.

VAULTS
A post at Chillon Castle, France, has an iron ring attached, to which prisoners were manacled to prevent them from escaping.

VICTIM?
This picture shows Edward V with his parents Edward IV and Elizabeth Woodville.

DEATH BY BURNING
Those who refused to follow the state religion were sometimes burned at the stake. Many burnings took place during the 16th century.

Banner bearing fleur-de-lis, the traditional heraldic symbol of France

MAID OF ORLEANS
This 19th-century statue is of Joan of Arc, a young Frenchwoman from Orleans who was burned at the stake for witchcraft in 1431 because of her leading role in victories over the English. She was imprisoned in the castle at Rouen during her trial.

OFF WITH HIS HEAD!
The sword was used in Europe for beheading, as in this 15th-century picture. The victim waits blindfolded for the fatal blow.

Sturdy grille made of hardwood

Wooden peg

Window

Stone bench seat

Small wooden door for passing food and drink to prisoner inside

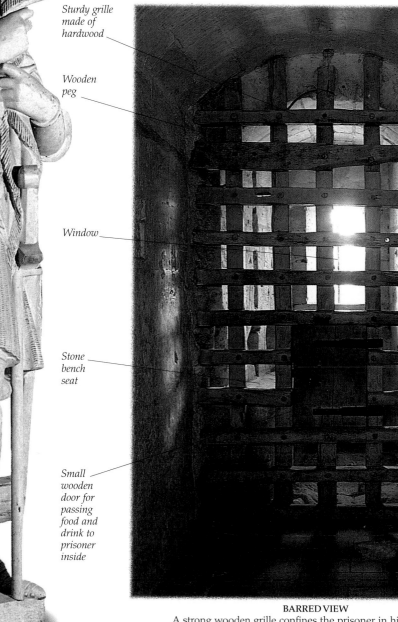

BARRED VIEW
A strong wooden grille confines the prisoner in his room in the castle at Loches. Prisoners were often allowed to have much more space than in this small cell.

Crusader castles

FOR MORE THAN 200 YEARS European Christians fought the Muslims to try to win control of the Holy Land by launching expeditions called crusades. They were impressed by huge Byzantine and Muslim fortifications and took over Muslim strongholds to encourage European settlers. They built castles to guard roads and to help them attack nearby towns. By the late 12th century such castles were being used as border posts, administrative centers, safe havens, and army bases. Often, the crusaders used good sites for castles, places protected on three sides by a sea or river; they built strong walls and ditches to guard the fourth side. Elsewhere, rapid building was necessary, so simple rectangular enclosures with corner and flanking towers appeared.

BESIEGED
This 13th-century Italian manuscript shows crusaders trying to break into Antioch. This city was so large that the men of the First Crusade (1095–1099) could not surround it, in spite of the size of their army. So they had to guard against sorties from the gates, building forts to watch over them. European artists knew that the crescent was a Muslim symbol, and thought it was used on the defenders' shields.

MAILED KNIGHT
Crusaders, like this knight of about 1280, wore a shirt of mail, a cloth surcoat, and a helm on the head.

POOR KNIGHTS?
The seal of the Knights Templar shows two knights on one horse, suggesting their original poverty. This order of warrior-monks was formed in 1118. They took their name from their headquarters, which was near the Temple in Jerusalem.

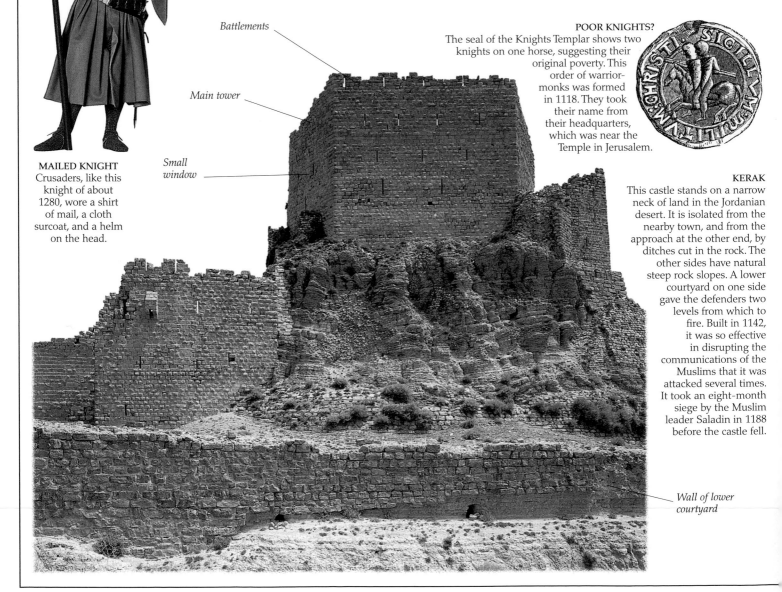

Battlements

Main tower

Small window

KERAK
This castle stands on a narrow neck of land in the Jordanian desert. It is isolated from the nearby town, and from the approach at the other end, by ditches cut in the rock. The other sides have natural steep rock slopes. A lower courtyard on one side gave the defenders two levels from which to fire. Built in 1142, it was so effective in disrupting the communications of the Muslims that it was attacked several times. It took an eight-month siege by the Muslim leader Saladin in 1188 before the castle fell.

Wall of lower courtyard

Angled talus (sloping wall)

High inner walls close to outer walls enable defenders to direct two lines of fire on enemy

High flanking tower

Commander's quarters

HOSPITALLER STRONGHOLD
Krak des Chevaliers in Syria was a small Arab fortress that was rebuilt in the 12th century by the Knights Hospitaller, the other great order of warrior monks. The rectangular castle was given an outer ring of walls to make a complex structure that withstood many sieges.

Outer curtain wall

Aqueduct to channel water into castle

CHARGE!
This Italian picture of a Turkish warrior dates from the early 16th century. In 1483 the Turks besieged and captured Constantinople, and in 1683 they reached the gates of Vienna in present-day Austria.

FALL OF JERUSALEM
The First Crusade finally reached Jerusalem in 1099. Breaking into the city after a siege, the soldiers began killing and looting. This picture of the fall of the city was made during the 15th century, hence the later style of armor worn by the soldiers.

16th-century Turkish soldier

MUSLIM FORTRESS *below*
The castle at Qatrana, Jordan, shows one typical design of fortification built by the Muslims after the departure of the crusaders. It was built using local limestone and its defensive features include machicolations and V-shaped arrow slits.

Machicolations protecting doorway

Cone-shaped crenellations

Narrow arrow slits

Decorative carved stone spheres

Castles in Japan

FORTRESSES HAD BEEN BUILT in Japan since the Yamato period (300–710 CE). Sometimes these were temporary strongholds, but by the 14th century more permanent fortifications of wood were beginning to appear. The 16th and early 17th centuries, a time when castles were in decline in Europe, saw the heyday of castles in Japan. The reasons for this were the political instability in Japan and the use of small firearms. Cannons were not highly developed there, so warriors could shelter behind castle walls, safe against the handguns and cavalry of their enemies. Natural hill sites were used if possible; otherwise, platforms of rammed earth were built and faced with dressed stone blocks. Rivers, lakes, or the sea provided natural moats.

MANY BAILEYS
Castles often contained many courtyards, which kept the main tower a safe distance from attempts to set it on fire. Progress through the courtyards was sometimes like going through a maze. An attacker would have to go through all the baileys before getting to the main tower.

NEW MONEY
Ieyasu was the first of the Tokugawa Shoguns, Imperial officials who became the most powerful men in Japan. He reorganized Japan's monetary system in the late 16th century. Cast or beaten slabs of gold or silver were used for coins.

Silver coin, 1601

Gold coin, 1601

SWORD POLISHING
Polishers work on lethally sharp samurai weapons. In the later 16th century, samurai warriors often lived in large castles, as the daimyos (provincial rulers) began to replace their many small fortresses with single huge castles, often built in towns. Such castles became administrative centers as well as fortresses.

SAMURAI
The samurai was in many ways similar to the feudal knight of Europe. He was a trained warrior who served a lord and expected to be served by peasants and merchants. His armor was made in a unique way. It consisted of iron plates laced together. Because of the damp climate, the iron was lacquered to stop it from rusting. This armor was effective against the very sharp swords used, which were the mark of the samurai. This picture shows a samurai warrior crossing the Uji River in 1184.

ATTACKING THE GATE
The assault on the Sanjo Palace (1160) shows a common method of attack. This was rarely successful, unlike starvation or betrayal. Sometimes the garrison shot the attackers in the courtyard. Siege techniques were similar to those used in Europe, although mines were not used until the later 16th century.

BADGE
Family badges were known as "mon." They were painted on items such as armor and banners. This is the butterfly mon of the Ashikaga family.

Highly decorated gable indicates the great power of the lord

LAYERED TOWER
There were often several towers in a castle, to allow the defenders to fire on the enemy from different angles. The gates also often had single-story towers over them. The heart of the castle was the main tower, which, built on an earthen mound, was several stories high. In later castles the base was protected by stone, while the structure above was made of wood. To reduce the fire risk, wooden parts of the towers were often thickly plastered and the gates covered with iron plates. Towers like this one at Himeji Castle served as command centers, watchtowers, and storage areas. In the upper floors were quarters for the lord.

Wooden upper story

Pagoda-like roof with broad overhang

Narrow window openings

Roof of wooden shingles

Plastered outer wall

Inner framework of timbers

Gun loop

Ground floor protected by dressed stone slabs

37

The great hall

THE HALL WAS the main room in European castles. It was used for eating, sleeping, and carrying out castle business. The day in the hall began early with breakfast, which consisted of bread soaked in ale or watered wine, eaten after Mass. The main meal, where formality and good manners were expected, was eaten at about ten or eleven in the morning. In the evening there were various suppers, which often ended in overeating and drunkenness. Servants with ewer, basin, and napkin poured water over the hands of important guests before and after meals; other people washed at basins near the doors. Later the trestles were removed to make room for entertainment and eventually the stuffed palliasses used for sleeping. Only rich people had real beds. During the 13th century the lord began to distance himself from the larger household, and extra rooms were built for him and his close family.

12th-century copper-alloy hanging lamp

Holder for candle

Modern drip-catcher

FLOORED!

A 13th-century tile illustrates the legend of Tristan, one of the Knights of the Round Table. The floors of royal palaces, rich halls, and abbeys were decorated with many tiles like this. Carpets were imported as luxuries from the East, but they were usually hung on the walls, like tapestries.

HEARTH AND HOME

Early halls had a fireplace in the middle of the room, but these were later abandoned in favor of wall fireplaces, which had the advantage of a flue to carry away the smoke. The lord's table was often near the fire for warmth and was placed at one end so the lord could survey the whole hall. Often on a raised platform or dais, it might be the only table with fixed legs and a cloth.

Silver bird holds shield with heraldic arms of the Count of Flanders

Gilded mount

Maple-wood cover

Bowl made from very finely cut maple wood

Animal decoration

Decorative enameled lozenge

CANDLESTICK

Animals and plants decorate this late 12th-century copper-alloy German candlestick. Candles were made from animal fats. Oil lamps were also used.

CHEERS!

Wooden covered bowls were sometimes used for drinking toasts. They were called mazers, from an old word for maple, the wood used to make the bowls. This rich 15th-century Flemish example has a gilded silver foot. It probably belonged to Louis de Male, Count of Flanders. Other precious vessels in the hall included the salt cellar. This was placed in front of the principal guest at mealtimes; smaller "salts" were placed on other tables. Lesser folk sat "below the salt."

ROYAL HALL
Steps from the hall at Loches, France, led out to the battlements, marked by the round tower. Often the curtain wall formed one side of the hall. This saved money on building, but large windows could not be pierced on this side of the hall. Early halls had been made of timber, but stone became increasingly common. Because of the smell and fire risk, the lord usually built his hall well away from the castle kitchen.

FORMAL MEALS
These took place in the great hall. Sometimes there was a lesser hall where the castle constable conducted business.

STEEP ROOF
The castle at Loches on the Loire River in France has a keep of the 11th and 12th centuries with many later additions. The royal hall with its stepped gable is associated with the 15th-century king Charles VII, whose mistress Agnès Sorel lived at Loches and is buried there.

Battlements of great hall

Conical, slate-covered roof

Door to tower and outer courtyard

Circular tower overlooks battlements, to give a good view of the surrounding area

Large upper windows of great hall

The kitchen

HOOKING OUT THE FOOD
A 14th-century cook uses flesh-hooks to manhandle pieces of meat.

IN THE MIDDLE AGES, the heat for cooking was provided by fires. Accidental fires could be disastrous, so the castle kitchen was often housed in a separate building in the courtyard. But this meant that the food cooled as it was carried to the table. So it became more common for the kitchen to be joined to the castle hall by a passage. It might contain an open hearth or ovens set into the walls. In addition there could be a range of other rooms nearby—a pantry (for storing food), a buttery (for bottles), a bakehouse, and perhaps even a brewhouse with a tank to soak barley and kilns to dry the grain to make beer.

Socket to take handle

Holes through which water could drain

SKIMMER
Many foods were cooked by boiling them in water. A tool like this skimmer could be used to remove small items from a cauldron. The hot water would drain away through the holes. There was originally a long wooden handle to prevent the cook's fingers from getting burned.

CORE OF THE PROBLEM
This object is probably an apple corer. It could be pushed into the middle of the apple to remove the core.

Hollow tube removes core, leaving the more edible parts

Wooden handle

LEGS TO STAND ON
Cooking pots with legs could stand right in the fire. The long handle helped to prevent burned fingers.

KNIFE
As today, knives of all sizes were used in the kitchen for cutting, carving, and boning.

FLESH-HOOK
This was a tool with metal prongs that were sometimes bent into hooks. Using the wooden handle, the flesh-hook could be thrust into a piece of meat to lift it into or out of a cauldron of boiling water. This was a common way of cooking meat.

Hooked prong

SPITTED
In this 14th-century picture, several animals are turned on a spit so that they roast evenly. The man on the left puts a log on the fire using a long forked stick.

CLEAVER
The cook would cut up animal carcasses with a cleaver. It had a large, deep blade, because it was brought down through the meat like an ax. The weight of the blade, as well as its sharp, curved edge, helped to cut through the flesh.

SUGAR LOAVES
White sugar was a costly rarity in Europe—it had to be brought from the East. The lowest quality of refined sugar was the conical loaf shown here, which was made from white paste. Powdered white sugar, sometimes flavored with spices or flowers, was a luxury. There was also brown sugar and molasses, which came from Sicily.

Chains to hang pot

Carrying handle

HANG IT
This flat-bottomed pot was hung over the fire, probably from a hook in the top of the fireplace.

Decorative animal's-head spout

Late-14th-century hairstyle

FASHIONABLE POT
By the 13th century, pots made of iron, bronze, or copper were gradually replacing those made from earthenware. Round-bottomed ones, like this bronze laver or cauldron, were designed to be hung from chains over a fire. This one has been livened up with moldings of animal faces. Each attachment for the hanging chain is shaped like a woman's face. The hairstyles help to date the pot to the late 14th century.

Spout in shape of animal's face

Broad, heavy blade

PITCHER
Many pitchers were made of pottery, often with the green glaze typical of medieval ware. In order to make them more attractive, potters sometimes molded faces or animals into the surface. Here, there is a decorative spout shaped like an animal's head.

At the table

A **VARIETY OF FOODS** were served in the castle hall. Beef and mutton were the main meat dishes, but venison was eaten after a successful hunt. Because there was no refrigeration, animals were kept near the kitchen until ready for slaughtering. Otherwise meat was salted to preserve it. Rich sauces were useful to disguise the taste of overripe meat in winter. Poultry and eggs were often eaten, wild birds of all kinds ended up on the menu, and game was popular. The meat might be eaten with onions, garlic, and herbs from the castle garden, and the most common vegetables were dried peas and beans. Fish was served on Wednesday, Friday, and Saturday, and also during Lent. Salted herring was common, but the castle fishponds provided freshwater species too. At feasts or royal meals, more exotic items, such as peacock or crane, were served. The most spectacular dish was the chef's subtlety, a mixture of sugar, paste, marzipan, and gelatin, painted and molded into shapes such as castles, ships, and hunting scenes.

Pheasant tail feather replaced after cooking

Plain, earthenware finish

Handle

WHAT A DISH
Some animals were made to look alive for presentation at the table—for example, by replacing feathers. Medieval people often liked their food to be artificially colored with fruit or vegetable juices.

DRINK, ANYONE?
Crude pottery jugs were used to carry ale or wine for the ordinary diners. Hops were unknown until the later Middle Ages, so beer was made from barley, wheat, oats, or a mixture of all three. Women known as alewives, or monks in monasteries, did the brewing.

FRUITFUL FARE
Castles often had walled gardens with orchards where fruit like this could be grown. Apples and pears grew in northern latitudes; farther south grew figs, grapes, oranges, and lemons.

Pewter plate

Pewter bowl with decorated edge

BOWL

This 12th-century bronze bowl is called a Hansa bowl. The Hansa was a league of North European trading towns and these bowls were widely used. Metal bowls were cleaned after use by boiling them in bran and then rubbing vigorously with a soft cloth.

Lid shaped like human face

HERE'S LOOKING AT YOU

The lid of this copper-alloy jug has been made with a face staring up, and the legs have feet shaped like animal paws. A jug like this might have contained hippocras, a drink made from wine mixed with honey and herbs.

Animal foot

BANQUET

Nobles were often served by pages who were training to become squires. In this 15th-century picture, most people sit on benches—only the rich used chairs. People had personal knives and spoons (pp.48–49), but forks were almost unknown. Often, two diners would share a bowl or even a cup.

PUDDING

This is an almond milk pudding. Milk was used mainly for cooking rather than drinking, and puddings like this were considered delicacies.

Rose petal

BREAD PLATES

Flat pieces of stale bread, called trenchers, were used as plates. They soaked up the gravy and, if uneaten afterward, could be given to the poor or thrown to the dogs. Whole-wheat bread was the most common and wastel was the finest white bread, eaten by the rich. Grain for the bread came from local manors and the bread was baked in the castle kitchen or bakehouse.

The entertainers

L<small>IFE IN A CASTLE</small> was not all work and warfare. Hunting and hawking were greatly enjoyed by all and brought useful additions for the table. Some outdoor pastimes were quite dangerous—there were tournaments for the knights, and bouts of wrestling or rough ball games. Adults even played children's games such as hoodman blind, when a person's head was covered and he or she had to chase the other players. To while away the hours indoors, people played board games and listened to musicians or storytellers. The storytellers recited the great heroic epics about knights such as Roland, troubadours in southern France sang of their love for ladies, and chivalric romances, such as tales of King Arthur's knights, were also popular. Much of this entertainment was provided by traveling minstrels and players, who moved around, but some kings and nobles kept a jester, or fool, to entertain them.

Hood to keep bird in the dark

GAMBLERS
Men often gambled at dice and became quite addicted to it.

Thick glove protects falconer from the bird's sharp talons

ROYAL PLEASURE
This lead badge shows a king riding with his falcon. All ranks of society enjoyed falconry, although some species of birds were reserved for the nobility. Falconry was a skill that had to be learned, but there was a great pleasure in working birds with a decoy bird (or lure) and watching their soaring flight and their ability to plummet down through the air (or stoop) to seize their prey.

Leather jesses keep bird on the fist

BIRD IN THE HAND
People often had a close relationship with their falcons. A lord might keep a falcon in his chamber, although they were usually kept in special buildings called mews. Some of the equipment used in falconry, such as the hood, came to Europe from the Middle East at the time of the Crusades.

HAWK BELLS
Bells were attached to the bird's leg so that the falconer knew where the creature was.

GARDENER'S WORLD
Castle gardens were usually well tended, not least because they grew herbs and fruit for the table. They were also pleasant places for lords and ladies to stroll and talk.

BEATING TIME

The more jolly medieval tunes had a strong drumbeat, which sometimes had quite a complex pattern. These small drums, in a picture from the mid-14th-century Luttrell Psalter, are called nakers. A very large drum was sometimes carried on the back while someone else struck it.

MINSTREL

A musician plays a hornpipe, so called because its wooden pipe is connected by a leather band to a hollowed-out cow's horn. Dancing, to the accompaniment of musicians playing instruments like this, was very popular. The earliest forms involved everyone holding hands in a ring or a long chain. Later there were more dances for couples. Minstrels also sang, sometimes accompanied only by the harp. Early songs often dealt with war; later love songs and those with a religious theme became popular. There were some songs that reminded people how Jerusalem was ruled by Muslims and urging Christian crusades to win it back.

Wooden pipe

Slashed sleeves

Leather band

Hollowed-out cow's horn

Checker-board pattern often worn by entertainers

Woolen hose

HURDY-GURDY

A 14th-century musician is playing a hurdy-gurdy. This was played by turning a handle that sounded all the strings at once to produce a drone-like sound. The fingers of the other hand were then used to produce the required notes.

WHAT A FOOL

The job of the fool or jester was to make people laugh. His jokes could be very crude. He might wear a cap and bells and carry a slapstick, a two-part stick that made a loud noise. He was sometimes allowed to say things to his master that others dared not.

BALL GAMES

This 15th-century ball game with curved sticks may be an early version of field hockey. The ball used was quite large and was probably made of leather.

Women and children

THE MOST IMPORTANT woman in the castle was the lady, the wife of the lord. The families of knights might also live in the castle, and the children of other lords might be trained there. High-ranking women had their own ladies-in-waiting to attend them, and there were also female servants. Laundresses cleaned soiled clothing and seamstresses repaired it. Women of all classes learned how to spin, weave, and sew, and some ladies of rank were skilled at embroidering in gold and silver threads.

HIGH AND LOW
This 15th-century picture of a well-dressed lady and a female laborer shows the differences in the classes of society. The peasant is shown, as often in pictures, digging with her back bent.

SIDE SADDLE
The Wife of Bath, from Geoffrey Chaucer's late 14th-century *Canterbury Tales*, had been married several times and showed that women sometimes had a degree of independence.

HEAD OF STONE
This 14th-century stone corbel, carved to represent a woman, once jutted from a wall to take the weight of an arch or beam. The woman wears a wimple, a piece of linen that passed under the chin. The wimple was popular throughout the Middle Ages and was often worn with a veil. Married women often covered their hair as a mark of their position and age.

Wimple, fastened to the hair by pins

Veil

PLAYING SOLDIERS
This little metal toy sword and helmet are copies of full-size items used in war. They were probably played with by young boys who might one day use real arms in battle.

Sword

Helmet

Children

When only about seven, a boy from a noble family might be sent to a castle, often that of a relative, to become a page and learn good manners. After about seven years he would begin to train as a squire, perhaps being knighted when about 21. Girls were also sent to another castle to be taught by the lady in the arts of sewing, homemaking, and how to behave correctly—especially in front of the gentlemen.

BRINGING UP BABY
Childbirth was often dangerous, for medical knowledge in the Middle Ages was limited and standards of hygiene were low. Many mothers and babies died, but families were still often large. Noblewomen sometimes gave their babies to wet nurses to breastfeed rather than doing this themselves.

TOGETHERNESS

Knights and nobles often married an heiress for her land. In spite of this inauspicious start, couples often grew close. People of lower rank had a wider choice of partners, although anyone with a lord normally had to get his permission to marry.

Sapphire *Ruby*

Amethyst

English cross-brooch

Late 13th-century English gilt brooch

THE LADY

This lady of the early 15th century would run the household in her husband's absence and check his nearby manors. She also had to entertain visitors to the castle, greeting them at the gate and being there to say farewell. She was in charge of the castle kitchens and the menu, although she would not normally cook the food herself. In her spare time she would enjoy hunting, dancing, and playing chess and other board games.

SIGNS OF WEALTH

Ladies liked to wear costly jewelry— because it looked attractive, because of its fine workmanship, and because it showed how rich they were.

HARD SOLE

Pattens had solid, raised wooden soles and could be slipped over ordinary leather shoes if the weather was bad. They were useful when rain made tracks and roads very muddy.

Leather strap

Solid wooden sole

CHRISTINE DE PISAN

This well-educated woman wrote poems and other works in the late 14th century and became a professional writer in the early 15th century.

Padded roll over net

Plackart

Kirtle

Tight-fitting sleeve

Sideless surcoat

Train

The lord

KING'S COIN
This gold coin is
a bulla, made for
Edmund, King
of Sicily.

A CASTLE WAS HOME TO A LORD, who could be anyone from a minor baron to the king himself. A large castle could be used as an administrative base by a powerful lord, who could also live there in comfort. The lord's rank meant that he enjoyed the luxury of privacy, with his own chamber. Kings and great lords, who had several castles and houses, would appoint an official called a castellan to run the castle in their absence. But if during a siege the castellan felt it necessary to surrender, the laws of war said that he should first send word to his lord for permission to do so. The king would also entrust some of his castles to local officials such as sheriffs, who governed part of the country using the castle as a base. Such castles were usually built in towns and would often be connected to the town walls.

Dogs like greyhounds were valued hunting companions

HOMECOMING
A 14th-century knight returns home. He is wearing a large steel helmet called a basinet. Lookouts watch from their lofty perch in a high tower.

PERSONAL ITEMS
A lord would usually have his own cutlery, which might be kept in a leather case. These are two of a set of four knives that are decorated with the heraldic arms of John the Fearless, Duke of Burgundy.

HAT TRICK
This lord wears a chaperon, a distinctive 15th-century hat. It developed from the hood, with the face-opening worn on the top of the head. The long "tail," originally the back of the hood, is called a liripipe.

Carving knife

Eating knife

Enameled arms, used between 1371 and 1404

STAYING IN SHAPE
The lord was a knight and was expected to fight for his king if necessary. Many practiced by taking part in tournaments, where mounted knights fought in front of admiring ladies. Knights could enter either the team game (the tourney) or single combat with lances (the joust). In this 15th-century picture, two knights have shattered their lances against one another and are fighting with swords.

IVORY CASKET
Caskets contained personal possessions and came in various sizes. This French example is made from ivory and is carved with scenes from the anonymously-written 13th century romantic novel *Chateleine de Vergy*. It was made in the second quarter of the 14th century.

DISPLAY
Lords displayed their wealth not only on themselves but also on their family and retainers. This early 15th-century buckle, found at Chalcis in Greece, is made of silver.

THE LORD
Men who ran small castles, particularly in the unsettled period between the 10th and 12th centuries, were not always too fussy about their dress. But those in charge of larger castles were often eager to impress with the richness of their clothes, especially on formal occasions such as feasts or a royal visit. This 15th-century lord wears a long formal gown called a houppelande.

Collar of doublet worn under gown

Collar with badge

Pendant with badge

Linen shirt

Gilt decoration covering silver metal

Full sleeves

Belt carrying purse

Velvet gown

Silver

Woolen hose

UNDERWEAR
In the 14th and 15th centuries a man would wear a doublet beneath his gown. Under the doublet was a shirt. In contrast to the outer garments, the shirt was quite plain and functional. Because it was worn next to the skin, it was made of linen, to prevent itching. Woolen hose would be attached to the lower edge of the doublet by small laces called points.

Pointed leather shoes

SHOWING OFF
This early 14th-century mount is made from gilt silver and was worn on a belt. Like the buckle at the top of this page, it was found at Chalcis in Greece.

Fabrics and textiles

IN THE MEDIEVAL PERIOD people usually made their own clothes, either spinning and weaving the cloth themselves, or buying linen in large amounts and making up garments when needed. Wool was the most common textile, and was often woven with goat's hair to make chamlet, an ideal material for making clothes. The rich might wear garments of more expensive cloths, such as linen or silk. Everyone wore underclothes of linen, because they were comfortable next to the skin. Varieties of silk increased during the Middle Ages, with types called samite, damask (from Damascus), and taffeta becoming available.

DYEING FOR A LIVING
Cloth could be colored by soaking it in a tub filled with a natural dye. Such dyes were usually made by boiling the roots or leaves of certain plants in water. Buttermilk (the liquid fat left after making butter) was a useful whitener.

Wooden distaff

Thread

Fleece

Whorl

Ball of woolen thread

WORKING WITH WOOL
Once sheared from the sheep and washed, the fleece was carded—stroked with a toothed tool to untangle it and make the strands point in one direction. These strands were then wound around a distaff and fingerfuls of wool pulled away and twisted into a thread.

Sprung rounded end

Blade

Cloth shears

Sharp inner edge

Shearing shears

CUTTING UP
Wool was sheared from the sheep using large shears. Smaller versions would be used to cut the cloth. Unlike scissors, which have two arms that pivot at the center, the arms of shears are joined at one end and they cut when the two arms are pressed together so that the blades slide over each other. The rounded end of the shears is springy, and the blades open automatically when released.

Steel blade

Distaff

Leatherworking

Shoes, saddles, clothing, scabbards, belts, and straps for pieces of armor were just some of the items made from leather. Molded leather was even used to make pieces of armor, as an alternative to steel. It was also used to make jugs and buckets. Many leather objects were skillfully decorated with cut, pricked, or molded designs.

AT WORK
This 15th-century picture shows leatherworkers at their trade.

SHARP BLADE
This knife was used for cutting through hide. The leatherworker moved the handle back and forward so that the whole blade sliced through the leather. Leatherworkers still use tools like this today.

Pushing this large
wheel around makes
the distaff turn

Drive thread
connects distaff
with large wheel

Worker's hand
pulls fleece out
into a thread

Fleece

SPINNING A YARN
Most girls and women were taught
to spin. This 14th-century woman
is using a spindle wheel. With this
device, a push of the large wheel keeps
the distaff turning, so that the yarn winds on
to it as it is pulled out into a thread. This technique could be
used to produce different grades of yarn. Coarse wool, such as
blachet, was used for items like bed covers. The coarsest types,
russets and burels, were used mostly by the poor. Woolen yarn
was woven into cloth on a loom. Knitting only began in the 15th
century and in some places only became a craft a century later.

In the fields

SOWING
Seed was carried in a bag or pouch and scattered over the soil by hand. Birds often managed to take some of the seed for themselves.

THE PEOPLE WHO LIVED and worked in a castle had to eat, and horses and hunting dogs had to be fed. Much of the food was grown in the surrounding fields, which belonged to the lord of the castle. The workers who tilled these fields lived in villages nearby. In times of trouble they and their animals could seek shelter within the castle walls. Producing food was hard work in the Middle Ages. It meant getting up very early in all weathers, at all times of the year, in order to plow the fields, sow the seed, and harvest the crops in fall. In sunny areas vines were grown to produce wine. Beer brewed from barley was popular in northern Europe; the water was so dirty that drinking it could make people very ill.

PRUNING
In March the vines were pruned with a short-handled billhook, which could cut the branches back to ensure good growth.

PLOWING
The iron plowshare turned over a furrow in the earth ready for planting crops. Usually the plow was pulled by oxen. Eight animals were sometimes used, but generally it was four or less, as shown on this 14th-century tile. The peasants pooled their livestock to provide enough animals to pull the plow.

SICKLE
The sickle was used to cut crops in July, the stalks being left half-cut to provide straw for cattle. The wheat or barley would then be threshed to separate out the grain, which the miller ground down to make flour for breadmaking.

Ears and grains of emmer wheat

Iron sickle

HEAVE!
This 14th-century haycart is being pushed uphill. Solid collars on the horses enabled them to pull without choking.

WINNOWING
This miniature, from the early 15th-century *Très riches heures* of the Duke of Berry in France, shows the month of June. It is represented by men using scythes to cut the hay and two women tossing up the hay to winnow it. The hay provided winter fodder for cattle.

WINE

The vines are being carefully tended in this 15th-century Flemish picture. Once ripe, the grapes were picked and packed in large casks where barefoot workers trod them to squash out their juice. This was collected and left to ferment until it formed wine.

HARD WORK

This 15th-century illustration from the *Book of Hours* of the Duchess of Burgundy shows the task for March: hoeing the ground to break up the topsoil for planting.

AX

A multipurpose tool, the ax could be used for felling small trees, chopping up firewood, or cutting logs.

Ax head

"Beak"

BILLHOOK

This tool was used for pruning. It had a long cutting edge and a "beak."

PITCHING IN

The pitchfork had two prongs, called tines, and a long wooden shaft. It was mainly used for thrusting into sheaves, or bundles, of hay, and pitching them up onto a wagon.

Tine

SON OF THE SOIL

The peasant was not usually allowed to leave the land his family worked. He was a serf or villein, which for some was little different from being a slave, except that medieval peasants had to feed themselves from what they grew. The lord took a percentage of the crops for himself and the peasant had to grind grain in the lord's mill, for a price. A peasant's life was often very hard. He was dependent on the weather, and ruined crops meant famine. The Black Death killed many peasants in the 14th century and they became more valued by the upper classes as a result of this.

Leather cap

Coarse woolen tunic

Leather bag

Warm woolen hose

Tough leather boots for hard work

Animals in the castle

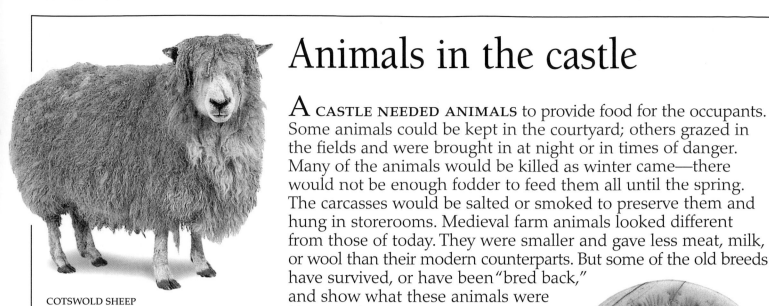

A CASTLE NEEDED ANIMALS to provide food for the occupants. Some animals could be kept in the courtyard; others grazed in the fields and were brought in at night or in times of danger. Many of the animals would be killed as winter came—there would not be enough fodder to feed them all until the spring. The carcasses would be salted or smoked to preserve them and hung in storerooms. Medieval farm animals looked different from those of today. They were smaller and gave less meat, milk, or wool than their modern counterparts. But some of the old breeds have survived, or have been "bred back," and show what these animals were like. To add variety to the table, wild animals were hunted as extra food.

COTSWOLD SHEEP
Medieval sheep were smaller and thinner than sheep today and their meat would probably have been less tender to eat. But they were very useful animals. Their skins were used to make parchment for writing on and their wool was vital for clothing. In the 15th century, English owners made fortunes by selling wool to make cloth.

SWEETENERS
Sugar was rare and expensive, so honey was often used for sweetening. These beekeepers use wickerwork beehives.

Hive (or bee skep) made of wickerwork

MONTH BY MONTH
This 12th-century ivory games counter is part of a set. Each one shows familiar country scenes that portray different months of the year.

Zodiac sign of Aries the Ram

January represented by a man carrying a bundle of sticks

Long, curved horns

BAGOT GOAT
Goats provided milk and were unpicky eaters in the castle courtyard. Bagot goats probably arrived in Europe in the 14th century, brought by crusaders returning from the Holy Land. Their name comes from Sir John Bagot, to whose park they were presented. In 1380, a goat's head was added to the Bagot family's coat-of-arms.

FRESH EGGS
Chickens could be left to scratch around inside the castle courtyard. They might be tied to a peg to stop them from wandering.

PORKER
Medieval pigs, like those before them, were much more like wild boars in shape and were nowhere near as fat as modern pigs. In medieval England they were not only useful for providing pork, they were sometimes trained as retrievers, like modern dogs, and were used when poaching.

Dark, hairy skin, like that of a wild boar

CONEY
Rabbits were caught for food, and for their fur, which was called coney. A ferret was put down one hole and the rabbit caught in a net as it bolted out of another. Rabbit burrows or warrens were specially set up, and maintained by an official who was called a warrener.

PHEASANT
The Romans probably introduced pheasants to England. People hunted them with bows or falcons to provide a source of additional food.

PANNAGE
To overcome winter food shortages, pigs could be driven into the local woodland in November. Here, as this 15th-century picture shows, people knocked down acorns from oak trees for the pigs to eat. The pigs also liked beech nuts. The right to pasture pigs in a forest was known as pannage.

Attractive brindled coat

Wide horn span—horns were left uncut in the Middle Ages

Long, shaggy hair keeps goat warm in winter

Udder—cattle were a source of milk as well as meat

LONGHORN
Unlike the cattle of today, whose horns are usually removed for safety, medieval cattle could have very long horns indeed. Longhorn cattle may be descended from the wild cattle first domesticated in the Stone Age. Cattle provided meat, and their hides were tanned to make leather. The steers were harnessed to a plow by a wooden yoke (horses were not often used for this task). The cows were milked, as were ewes and she-goats.

The castle builders

ONCE A SUITABLE SITE with fresh water was found, the lord employed a master mason, often on contract, to help plan and build the castle. Such highly respected men would employ a clerk to keep the accounts and obtain building materials. The master mason would take charge of the building work. Under him were an army of workers. Hewers cut the stone at the quarry; freemasons cut the fine blocks of building stone (known as ashlar) and carved decorative moldings; roughmasons and layers built the walls. There were many other workers doing specific jobs, from carpenters to well-diggers, smiths to stone-porters.

STONEWORK
A 13th-century mason wearing a cloth coif on his head shapes stone blocks while a basket of stone is sent up to the workman waiting at the top of the building.

CROWBAR
Heavy blocks of stone needed to be manhandled from quarry to building site and into their final position.

CHISELING IT OUT
From the 12th century onward, chisels were used more and more, replacing axes for stone-cutting. Masons used a mallet and chisel to carve decorative designs into stone.

DIVIDERS
By setting a distance between the two arms, dividers could be "walked" across a piece of stone to fix a measurement. They could also be used like a compass, to scribe circles or curves.

MEN AT WORK
Workers supply stone blocks using a wooden ramp and a type of wheelbarrow. Often rough stone-and-mortar walls were faced with ashlar. If the whole wall was not faced, ashlar would be put around doors, windows, and loopholes.

TROWEL
Mortar was mixed and laid on with a trowel. It was made by mixing sand and lime; the latter was sometimes provided by burning limestone on site. Mortar bound together the rubble walls of rough stone and the fine ashlar facings. It was also used in building the brick castles that appeared in the later Middle Ages.

SHAPING UP
Shaping stones was skilled work. A 15th-century mason inspects a fine squared stone block to be sure it will fit.

Measuring arm

MASON'S CHISEL
Chisels were used for cutting and dressing stone, although some stone was soft enough to be cut with a saw. A smithy was needed on site because the tools wore out quickly.

STRAIGHT MAN
A lord talks with his master mason, who carries a plumb line. The lead weight on the end keeps the line hanging straight down, in order to check verticals.

Plumb line

COUCY-LE-CHATEAU
This is a model of the great tower of Coucy-le-Chateau at Aisne in France. It was built between 1225 and 1242 by Duke Enguerrand III. The tower was very strongly built, with great arches intersecting in the middle. Even if an enemy broke into one of the niches, the wall arch around it would prevent the stonework from collapsing.

Window with stepped opening

Fireplace with chimney built into wall

Entrance to great tower

Stone arched bridge to castle entrance

VAULT
In order to carry the weight of a stone roof, builders of the Norman period used a tunnel effect called a barrel vault. By crossing two of these at right angles, a groined vault was made. Here we see the outer part of the vault as it rises upward from a corner.

Groin

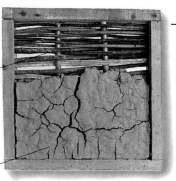

Wattle (interwoven branches)

Daub (a mixture of straw, mud, and manure)

WATTLE AND DAUB
Many of the buildings in a castle courtyard might be timber-framed. The gaps between the wooden uprights were often filled with panels of interwoven branches (or wattle), plastered with daub, a mixture of straw, mud, and manure.

Parapet to protect soldiers on gallery

Gallery

Passageway within thick outer walls of great tower

PULLEY
A 13th-century mason uses a pulley to haul up a basket full of stone.

Moat

The woodworkers

WOODEN CASTLES were far more common than those of stone before the 12th century. Professional woodworkers were needed to cut the timbers for palisade fences and walkways, the gate tower, motte tower, bailey buildings, and sometimes facings (called revetments) covering the slope of the motte and the bailey ditch banks. When stone castles became popular, some of the defenses might still be made of wood. In addition, large amounts of wooden scaffolding were needed as the building rose up. Courtyard buildings were often made of wood or built with a wooden frame. Even in stone buildings, wood was used for roof and ceiling beams and floors. Inside, carpenters made doors, shutters, partitions, paneling, and furniture. They would also make catapults and other engines (see pp.24–25) to help defend the castle during a siege.

HOARDINGS
Removable wooden hoardings were supported on beams pushed into holes below the battlements.

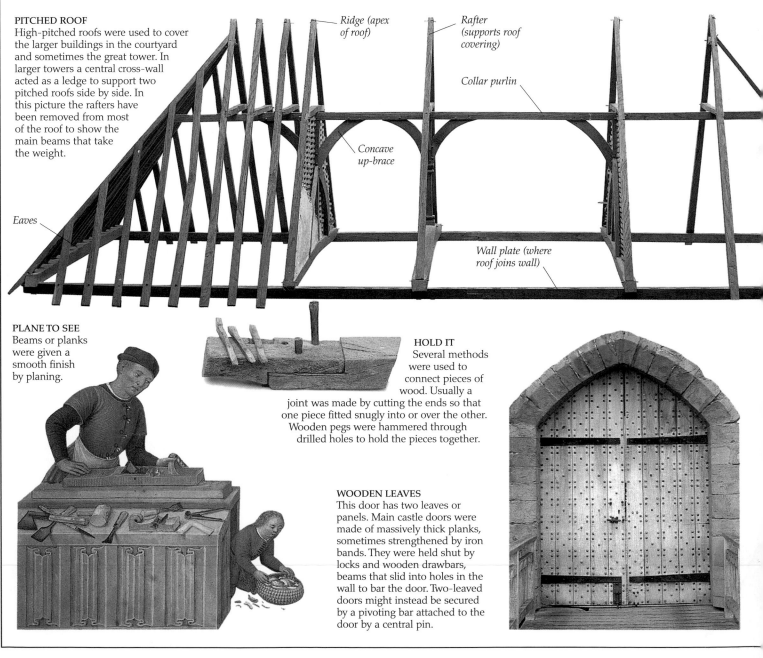

PITCHED ROOF
High-pitched roofs were used to cover the larger buildings in the courtyard and sometimes the great tower. In larger towers a central cross-wall acted as a ledge to support two pitched roofs side by side. In this picture the rafters have been removed from most of the roof to show the main beams that take the weight.

Eaves

Ridge (apex of roof)

Rafter (supports roof covering)

Collar purlin

Concave up-brace

Wall plate (where roof joins wall)

PLANE TO SEE
Beams or planks were given a smooth finish by planing.

HOLD IT
Several methods were used to connect pieces of wood. Usually a joint was made by cutting the ends so that one piece fitted snugly into or over the other. Wooden pegs were hammered through drilled holes to hold the pieces together.

WOODEN LEAVES
This door has two leaves or panels. Main castle doors were made of massively thick planks, sometimes strengthened by iron bands. They were held shut by locks and wooden drawbars, beams that slid into holes in the wall to bar the door. Two-leaved doors might instead be secured by a pivoting bar attached to the door by a central pin.

BAD WORKER
This early 14th-century tile from Tring, England, shows a master craftsman telling off a worker for cutting a beam too short. Workers of various professions were organized into guilds, with rules and standards of quality to be kept up.

SAW POINT
These sawyers are cutting a large piece of wood with a two-handed saw. Sometimes a saw-pit was used, the lower-ranking man standing in the pit, where he was showered with shavings.

Auger

Hammer

TOOLS OF THE TRADE
The tools used by medieval carpenters were very similar to those of today. The auger was twisted around to bore holes; the hand saw cut small pieces of wood. The metal parts were made by a smith (pp.60–61).

Hand saw

CARPENTER
Skilled woodworkers were always in demand because of the large number of objects made from this material. Unlike today, large areas of countryside were covered in woodland and forest, and lumber was carefully managed to make sure supplies were always on hand. Once a castle was built, there was always need for a carpenter to repair or replace damaged items, or woodwork damaged by insects, fungus, or rot.

Tie-beam

Awls

Billhook

Broad ax

Adze (for cutting slivers from the surface)

Chisel

Metalwork

CLOSE WORK
If a seamstress needed a thimble to protect her finger, a metalworker had to make it. This one might have been bought from a market, a shop, or a traveling merchant.

STRIKING A POSE
The smiths in this 15th-century manuscript are busily hammering metal into shape over a solid iron anvil, their tools hanging behind them. Some anvils had a "beak" at one end, which was used to shape metal objects like horseshoes, but the anvil used by armorers was often a simple cube of iron. Most smiths' workshops were housed in a separate building to reduce the risk of setting the rest of the castle on fire.

METALS OF ALL KINDS were used in castles. Iron was needed for a number of different everyday things, from horseshoes and harnesses to parts for siege engines, door hinges, tools, and hoops for barrels. Nails, both large and small, were used by the thousand for joining wood to construct palisades, wooden buildings, and parts of buildings such as roofs and doors. All these items had to be made by a metalworker (or smith) in the castle itself. The lord would frequently buy armor for himself and his knights from local merchants. A rich lord might even have some of his armor made abroad. But weapons and armor were in constant use. They were damaged in training and rivets would work loose. The castle armorer repaired damaged equipment.

Cutting edge

A SNIP
Snips were for cutting sheets of metal to give a basic shape to work on.

HOLD ON
Tongs were for holding metal when it was being hammered, especially when it was red-hot.

ARMED AND DANGEROUS
Armor and weapons like those of this 16th-century knight were often damaged in battle or tournament. An armorer who could do repairs, replace loose or broken rivets, and make pieces of mail and plate armor when needed was a valuable asset in a castle.

Metal tools

These medieval tools are little different from those used today. Armorers had extra tools, such as a huge pair of snips, set with one end fixed to a block, to cut sheets of steel for making plate armor.

NIPPERS
The pincers could cut through wire. They have a pivoting loop handle to hold them closed.

Handles

Swivel fastener

COPPER
A smith shapes copper in this 14th-century manuscript. Softer than other metals, copper was used for decorative work.

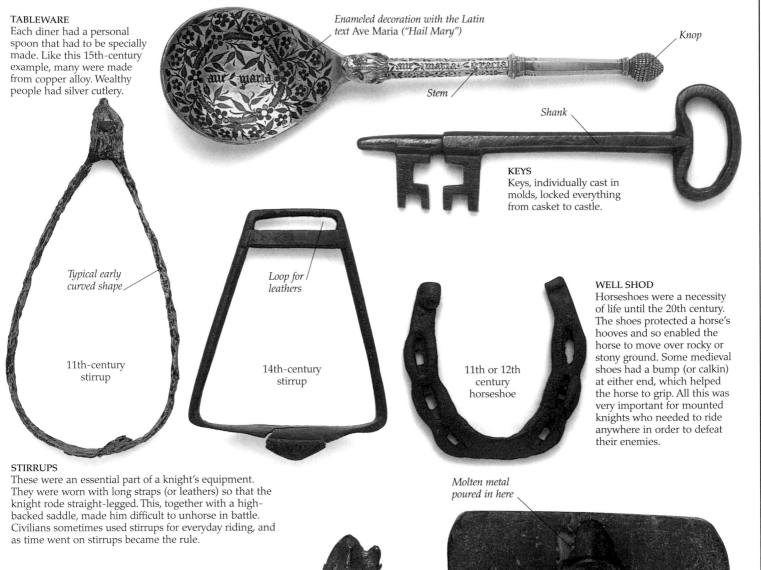

TABLEWARE
Each diner had a personal spoon that had to be specially made. Like this 15th-century example, many were made from copper alloy. Wealthy people had silver cutlery.

Enameled decoration with the Latin text Ave Maria ("Hail Mary")

Knop

Stem

Shank

KEYS
Keys, individually cast in molds, locked everything from casket to castle.

Typical early curved shape

Loop for leathers

WELL SHOD
Horseshoes were a necessity of life until the 20th century. The shoes protected a horse's hooves and so enabled the horse to move over rocky or stony ground. Some medieval shoes had a bump (or calkin) at either end, which helped the horse to grip. All this was very important for mounted knights who needed to ride anywhere in order to defeat their enemies.

11th-century stirrup

14th-century stirrup

11th or 12th century horseshoe

STIRRUPS
These were an essential part of a knight's equipment. They were worn with long straps (or leathers) so that the knight rode straight-legged. This, together with a high-backed saddle, made him difficult to unhorse in battle. Civilians sometimes used stirrups for everyday riding, and as time went on stirrups became the rule.

Molten metal poured in here

FORGE
This 19th-century picture of a forge shows that metalworkers were still using tools and techniques similar to those of their medieval counterparts.

MOLDED
Some items were made by melting metal and pouring it into a mold. This 15th-century figure is made from lead, which melts at a low temperature and was therefore easy to cast in this way. Lead was often used for making badges.

Figure

Mold

Castles in decline

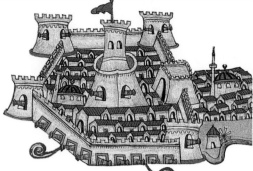

B**Y THE END OF THE 15TH CENTURY**, castles were losing their military importance. Societies gradually became more stable, and people demanded more comfortable living conditions. Gunpowder appeared in Europe in the early 14th century, but did not have a great effect on castles at first—they were still being built 200 years later. From the 16th century onward, some castles continued in military use, especially in danger areas like Austria, a buffer zone protecting western Europe from the Turks. Other castles were used as army barracks. Fortified tower-houses were still built in places such as Scotland, where riots or raids by neighbors made protection necessary. But many castles fell into ruin, their stones being stolen and used in buildings elsewhere. In the 18th and 19th centuries there was new interest in castles as symbols of the medieval world.

TURKS ATTACK
In 1453 the Turks managed to break into the heavily fortified city of Constantinople (now Istanbul), which was one of the last strongholds of the Christian Byzantine empire. The formidable walls were attacked by land and sea, and the Turks used numerous guns to make holes in the walls.

DEAL
The fort at Deal, England, was built by Henry VIII in the 1530s as part of a chain of similar defenses on the English coast. The low, rounded gun platforms present less of a target to cannon fire and deflect enemy missiles, but fortifications using arrowhead-shaped bastions were already taking over in Europe.

VASE GUN
The earliest pictures of cannons are English and appear in 1326. They show a vase-shaped object that would have been strapped down to a wooden stand. Such guns shot large metal darts and may have been aimed against doors to deter defenders from coming out.

Wooden tiller

Removable breech-block containing powder charge

Iron straps to secure barrel

Muzzle

CANNON
Huge guns called bombards were developed to blast walls with enormous stone balls. Smaller cannons, like this replica, were also increasingly used. This one has ropes for carrying, but by the 15th century some cannons had wheels.

Ropes for carrying

Notch in which to rest gun

Copy of late 14th-century handgun

Wooden pavise or portable shield

Heraldic badge to identify the lord of this marksman

Steel spike to stop shield from slipping

FAIRY-TALE CASTLE
The German castle of Neuschwanstein was built by King Ludwig of Bavaria in the late 19th century. It is one of several 19th-century castles created by people who were influenced by a romantic image of the medieval world.

Iron barrel

Steel kettle-hat

Coat-of-plates, a garment lined with steel plates riveted inside

Steel buckler or fist-shield

Wooden prop

HANDGUNNER
Early hand guns could be held behind a large shield and fired either by a hot wire pressed against the touch-hole, or by a glowing slow match made from cord soaked in saltpeter (potassium nitrate). Some guns had a lug on the bottom to hook over walls and absorb recoil. Inside a castle, guns could be fired through round loopholes in the walls or long horizontal slots for larger weapons, which could be fired at a besieger's cannons or earthworks. Later, guns were often arranged in groups, and this technique led to the building of forts designed to hold batteries of guns. Unlike medieval castles, these forts were usually built and run by the state.

Did you know?

FASCINATING FACTS

William the Conqueror

Kings provided their nobles with land on which to build castles. In return for this land, the nobles agreed either to provide the king with soldiers when he needed them or to pay a levy known as "shield money."

Peasants were completely controlled by their lord: they had to work for him, give him some of the produce they grew on their allotted land, pay to bake bread in his ovens, and remain on the same estate or submit to severe punishment.

Our word "slapstick," which means crude physical comedy, refers to a medieval jester's wand, a pair of sticks that made a loud noise when slapped together.

Jester

In the 13th century, some less affluent squires avoided becoming knights because they could not afford the specially trained horses and custom-made armor that went with the rank.

Practice battles, or tournaments, turned into popular entertainments in which single knights tried to knock one another off their horses (jousts), and teams of mounted knights engaged in mock combat (tourneys).

Neuschwanstein Castle

The famous Walt Disney logo was inspired by Neuschwanstein Castle in Germany. Dating from the late 19th century, it was designed (by a theatrical scene-painter) to look medieval.

Most people who lived in a castle slept where they worked—cooks in the kitchen, armorers in the armory, servants in the hall—but the lord and his family had their own quarters in a private, safe place such as a tower or gatehouse.

Krak des Chevaliers castle in Syria has a long, dark entrance passage. This ensured that any invaders who gained access would be temporarily blinded by the bright light when they finally emerged in the sun-drenched courtyard.

In 1204, soldiers attacking the fortress of Chateau-Gaillard in France gained entry by climbing up the lavatory shaft. A more common trick, and a more hygienic one, was to bribe one of the guards.

Castles were often altered by each generation: Windsor Castle, for example, was begun by King William I, then added to by Henry I and Henry II. Still a royal residence in the 21st century, it continues to undergo significant change and improvement.

One of the gatehouses at Caernarfon Castle in Wales was constructed with five doors and six portcullises.

While training to become knights, squires had to serve their lord at the table, care for his armor and dress him, tend his horses, assist him in battle, learn horsemanship and warfare, and train in sports such as wrestling and javelin throwing.

The original idea for concentric castles is likely to have come from knights who had been impressed with the double walls of Constantinople (Istanbul) when they fought there during the Crusades.

Lance

Jousting knight

Castles that were part of the fortifications around a town might be lived in by a sheriff or other official. These castles were part residence, part military barracks, part local government headquarters, and part prison.

Motte-and-bailey fortresses were extremely quick to construct: when William the Conqueror (William I) invaded England in 1066, he built castles at both Hastings and Dover in less than two weeks.

Many castles were built with secret tunnels leading outside so supplies could be smuggled in during a long siege.

QUESTIONS AND ANSWERS

Q Why were so many medieval castle towers round?

A Round towers allowed clearer sightlines for the defending forces inside. They also eliminated the structural weakness inherent in corners, where attackers would try to collapse the walls by tunneling underneath them (called undermining).

Q What part did castles play in national defense?

A No invading army could advance across a country's land without capturing every castle in its path—a prospect likely to deplete its numbers considerably. If they passed by these fortresses, the garrisons from each one could emerge, follow them, and attack from behind, or join together to form a large and powerful fighting unit.

Q Did most castles have dungeons and torture chambers underneath them?

A No, this is an element of castle life that—although not unheard-of—has been greatly exaggerated in books, plays, and movies. Since common criminals were usually punished with fines or execution, any castle prisoners were likely to be political, and therefore treated humanely. Also, we now know that many underground chambers once thought to be dungeons were actually drains. In some castles, though, dungeons were sometimes known as oubliettes, a word that suggests "locked away and forgotten."

Tintagel Castle

Q Was the legend of King Arthur and Camelot based on any real castle?

A Several locations have been suggested as the inspiration for these atmospheric tales of the Round Table. Among the most popular are Caerleon Castle in Wales, and Tintagel Castle and Cadbury Hill Castle in England.

Q Did medieval castle dwellers have real beds to sleep in?

A Most of the household slept on straw mattresses on the floor, but lords and ladies usually had elaborate wood-framed beds heavily draped against the cold. Tucked underneath, there was often a small "truckle" or "trundle" bed on wheels for children or servants.

Shield

RECORD BREAKERS

PROTECT AND DEFEND
The first castles (simple wooden structures) appeared in Europe during the 9th century, when wealthy nobles needed to defend their families and their lands against repeated attacks from Vikings and Magyars (invaders from present-day Hungary).

STRONG WALLS
The earliest known stone tower was erected at Doué-la-Fontaine, France, in about 950.

FORMIDABLE FORTRESS
The largest existing medieval castle is Hradcany Castle in Prague, Czech Republic. Originally built in the 9th century, it has been added to in some form during every era of its history. At the beginning of the 21st century, it still houses presidential offices.

MULTIPLE DEFENSES
One of the best-defended of all castles was Caerphilly Castle in Wales, which had concentric walls, multiple towers, two large lakes, and several moats and ditches. A complex system of tunnels and sluices controlled all the water levels.

Caerphilly Castle

Formal 15th-century robe called a houppelande

Who's who?

THE HOUSEHOLD OF A GREAT CASTLE could easily contain as many people as a small village: apart from the lord and his family, there would be officials, soldiers, indoor and outdoor servants and retainers, and even a small band of entertainers. During the 1400s, there were said to be over 400 indoor staff alone at Windsor Castle in England.

Castle lord

THE NOBLEMAN AND HIS FAMILY

THE CASTLE LORD, who held a noble title of some kind, was also a knight: a mounted warrior elevated to this rank by the king. He was sworn to serve the king, and to support him in battle, but he was also responsible for his own manor—his castle, his estate, and their communities.

THE LORD'S LADY, although she had no rights or property of her own, could wield considerable power, since she was responsible for things like keeping the household accounts, supervising the kitchens, entertaining important visitors, and raising the children. In her husband's absence, she would be in sole charge of the household.

CHILDREN of the lord and lady were usually sent away to another noble family when they were only about seven years old. There, the girls would be taught deportment and manners and given thorough instruction in spinning, sewing, and taking charge of a great household. Boys would become pages. Pages, too, learned courtly manners, but they also served at the lord's table and began training to become squires and—eventually—knights.

Younger sons, who would not inherit their father's estate, often went into the church, so they would never embark on the page-then-squire stages of training that led to knighthood.

OFFICIALS

THE CONSTABLE was the lord's second-in-command, and he would take overall charge of the castle when his master was away. In many castles, the constable was a relative of the lord. The constable was sometimes known as a CASTELLAN.

THE STEWARD was also very important; he kept the estate accounts, organized farm work, and presided at the manor court when the lord was away. The steward's role was enhanced considerably if his lord held several neighboring manors.

THE CHAMBERLAIN controlled the family's personal attendants, from ladies-in-waiting to lesser servants such as pages.

THE TREASURER collected rents and taxes and paid out wages and expenses.

THE BAILIFF allocated jobs to the peasants on the estate, cared for the livestock, and took responsibility for repairs to the castle and its outbuildings.

THE REEVE worked directly under the bailiff. He was a peasant: one of their own, chosen by the villagers to supervise them in their work.

THE CHAPLAIN was a priest who led worship in the castle chapel. The best-educated figure in the household (and often the only one who could read and write), he dealt with the lord's letters and paperwork and sometimes taught the lord's younger children as well.

Reeve

THE SHERIFF, a county official appointed by the king, represented police and local government rolled into one. The sheriff might use a castle—especially one that was part of a town's fortification—as his base when the lord was away. Some sheriffs were even castle lords in their own right.

A reeve's white stick was his badge of office.

SERVANTS

Manuscript illustration of ladies-in-waiting

LADIES-IN-WAITING were well-bred and educated women who acted as attendants to the lord's family.

PAGES AND SQUIRES, also of noble birth, performed personal services for the lord and his family such as carrying food to the top table during meals.

NURSES AND WET NURSES took full-time care of the infants and young children of the lord and lady.

DOMESTIC SERVANTS performed more menial tasks and often had specific areas of responsibility: women would be LAUNDRESSES, SEAMSTRESSES, SPINSTERS (who spun wool into thread), or WEAVERS, while men would be MASONS or CARPENTERS, providing everyday objects for use in the castle and keeping the structure in good repair. The GONG FARMER emptied the pit under each toilet.

KITCHEN STAFF, who were virtually all male, ranged from COOKS, BAKERS, PANTLERS (who took charge of the pantry, or dry-food store), BREWERS (who made beer), VINTNERS (who made wine), BOTTLERS, or BUTLERS (who took charge of the wine cellar), and TRENCHERMEN (who served up the food) to SCULLIONS (small boys who performed lowly tasks such as food preparation, dish washing, and turning the spit when a whole carcass was being roasted). Women sometimes brewed beer; they were called ALEWIVES.

OUTSIDE SERVANTS included STABLE GROOMS (who cared for the horses belonging to the lord and his knights), BLACKSMITHS (who made and repaired horseshoes and anything else fashioned from iron), ARMORERS (who mended and sometimes made weapons and armor), GARDENERS (who tended both the castle grounds and kitchen gardens), BEEKEEPERS (who provided honey for the kitchens), HUNTSMEN, WARRENERS (for hunting rabbits), and DOG-KEEPERS. FALCONERS played an important role, too, since falcons were widely valued as pets as well as for their skill in hunting.

RETAINERS were trusted older servants who had been part of a household for most of their lives. As a result, they were kept on and looked after by the lord even when they could no longer work full time, or even at all.

THE GARRISON

KNIGHTS led the body of men who lived in a castle in order to protect and defend it. They would often have their families with them. Each knight was served by a SQUIRE, who took care of his armor, his weapons, and his horse, and who was expected to come to his aid in battle.

HIRED SOLDIERS formed an important part of an area's defense force, especially as feudal services declined in the late 13th and 14th centuries. Many hired soldiers would fight on foot with either bows and arrows or staff weapons, such as axes, hammers, or blades mounted on poles. Cheaper to maintain than knights, hired soldiers eventually replaced them.

PRISONERS (either enemies of the lord or other noblemen being held for ransom) were occasionally locked up in castles, especially those castles that had dungeons underneath them.

HERALDS were soldiers who carried messages for their lord.

Knight and squire

ENTERTAINERS

Minstrel playing nakers (small drums)

MUSICIANS, sometimes including singers, might be employed permanently by wealthy lords to entertain his household and guests in the evenings and to provide music in the chapel. Some even had their own POETS, STORYTELLERS, and FOOLS or JESTERS, who wore amusing caps and bells and made people laugh by telling jokes.

TRAVELING PLAYERS would be taken on by castle households that did not maintain their own entertainers. Among these performers would be MINSTRELS and TROUBADOURS, who played music and sang, and MUMMERS, who formed companies or troupes to put on a repertoire of traditional plays.

Find out more

Perhaps the most exciting and romantic structures ever created, castles have the power to transport anyone who is enchanted by them into an exciting and magical bygone age. A surprising number of ancient castles are still standing and many are open to visitors, as well as being dealt with extensively in specialty books and websites. Many castles hold regular open days with experts available to provide information and entertainment, such as mock battles.

One of the most famous castles open to tourists is the Tower of London in England. Its imposing stone silhouette was originally a simple timber-and-earth structure erected by William the Conqueror. The principal residence for every English king from William II to Henry VII, four hundred years later, it has at some time been a fortress, a mint, a menagerie, an arsenal, a repository for the Crown Jewels (a role it still fulfills), a prison, and a place of execution.

White Tower

TOWER OF LONDON
Out of all the structures inside these historic castle walls, the White Tower dominates almost every view: from the air (above), or seen across the Thames River, behind Traitors' Gate (left). Covering an area of 107 x 118 ft (35 x 39 m), the White Tower contains the royal apartments and the Chapel of St. John.

Traitors' Gate (on the right), seen from the Thames River

Fantasy castles

Of all the castles that feature in popular fairy tales, novels, dramas, and games, many exist only in their creator's imagination, while some are based on real buildings.

• The sinister castle in Bram Stoker's nineteenth-century novel *Dracula* is said to be based on Bran Castle (also known as Castle Dracula), which is supposedly associated with Vlad Tepes, or Vlad Dracul, the 15th-century count who inspired the story. Bran Castle is in present-day Romania.

• Charles Perrault's classic 17th-century fairy tale *The Sleeping Beauty* was actually inspired by a castle: the 15th-century Château d'Ussé, whose turrets overlook the Indre River in western France.

• William Shakespeare set several of his plays in real castles: *Macbeth* takes place around Glamis Castle in Scotland, for example, while *Hamlet* inhabits Kronborg Castle in Denmark (Elsinore in the play).

Bran Castle towers above the town of Brasov

Bran Castle in Romania

Pont Sant' Angelo

CASTEL SANT' ANGELO
Along with its adjoining bridge, the Pont Sant' Angelo (above), this fortress takes its name from the Archangel Michael, who appeared to Pope Gregory the Great in the 6th century. At the time, Gregory was leading a procession across the bridge, praying for the end of the plague. Among the castle's interior treasures are a series of intriguing frescoes (left).

This fresco in Castel Sant' Angelo looks surprisingly real at first glance.

CHATEAU DE CHENONCEAU
Stretching out across the river Cher, Chenonceau has a 19-ft (60-m) gallery extending directly over the graceful arches that support the main structure. On the left is the 16th-century Turreted Pavilion, conceived by one of its early mistresses, Catherine Briçonnet, and built on the foundations of an old water mill.

USEFUL WEBSITES

- Castles Unlimited, a British conservation group
  www.castles-of-britain.com
- A list of links to American castles
  www.architecture.about.com/cs/castlesusa
- Site dedicated to German castles (including Neuschwanstein)
  www.mediaspec.com/castles
- Leeds Castle site
  www.leeds-castle.com
- Homepage of the Royal Armouries with links to collections at the Royal Armouries Museum in Leeds and the Tower of London
  www.royalarmouries.org
- History and explanation of the Bayeux Tapestry
  www.bayeuxtapestry.org.uk

Places to visit

TOWER OF LONDON, LONDON, ENGLAND
A World Heritage Site, the Tower is guarded by Yeoman Warders (popularly known as Beefeaters), who have performed this task since 1485, although their modern role is purely ceremonial. Of particular interest are:
• the White Tower, commissioned by William the Conqueror in 1078 and completed 20 years later
• Traitors' Gate, infamous as the portal used by political prisoners.

LEEDS CASTLE, KENT, ENGLAND
Another Norman fortress, moated Leeds Castle was a residence for six medieval queens, and served as one of Henry VIII's palaces. Among its attractions are:
• the impressively reconstructed royal rooms
• the quirky collection of dog collars dating back to the 16th century.

CAERNARFON CASTLE, GWYNEDD, WALES
Also a World Heritage Site, Caernarfon Castle is one of ten fortresses built in Wales by King Edward I. Edward II, the first Prince of Wales, was born here in 1284. Look for:
• the sites of the two Prince of Wales investitures held during the 20th century: those of George V's son (later Edward VIII) in 1911, and the present Prince of Wales in 1969.

CHATEAU DE CHENONCEAU, LOIRE VALLEY, FRANCE
Created and added on to by a number of powerful women between 1500 and 1800, Chenonceau is more like a pleasure palace than an armed fortress. Among its attractions are:
• the Turreted Pavilion created by 16th-century chatelaine Catherine Briçonnet
• the Grande Galerie, named for one of the castle's most famous ladies, Catherine de' Medici.

NEUSCHWANSTEIN CASTLE, BAVARIA, GERMANY
The ultimate in romantic fairy-tale castles, Neuschwanstein was built in the 19th century to look like a medieval palace. The improved technology of the time, however, made it considerably more comfortable. Its notable sites include:
• the wall paintings throughout the castle, which depict stirring scenes from German myth and legend
• the grand and gilded Throne Room with its exotic dome.

CASTEL SANT' ANGELO, ROME, ITALY
Connected to the Vatican Palace, the Castel Sant' Angelo was a medieval citadel and a place of safety for generations of popes. It also provides the theatrical last-act setting for Puccini's opera *Tosca*, in which the heroine jumps to her death from its round battlements. Among its historic features are:
• the Courtyard of Honor
• the Sala Paolina, with frescoes by Pellegrino Tibaldi and Perin del Vaga.

Glossary

Eighth-century keep at the ruins of a Moorish castle in Gibraltar

ARTILLERY Firearms such as cannons and handguns.

BAILEY Castle courtyard, often associated with a motte, as in motte-and-bailey castle. (*see also* MOTTE)

BARBICAN Outlying defense, usually in the form of a walled courtyard protecting a castle gate.

BARREL VAULT Half-barrel-shaped stone arch creating a stone ceiling.

BASTION Tower projecting from a castle wall.

BATTER Inclined face of a castle wall with a splayed-out base for increased stability. Also known as a TALUS.

BATTERING RAM Heavy beam used for breaching castle walls; sometimes decorated with ram's-head motif.

BATTLEMENT Parapet on top of castle walls where a soldier can stand to fire on attackers.

BOMBARD Cannon that fires huge stone balls.

BREWHOUSE Building or room where ale is brewed.

BUTTERY Room where food and drink are prepared and stored.

Cannonball for a bombard

CATAPULT Machine for hurling large rocks using the force produced by tension, torsion, or counterpoise.

CHIVALRY Moral, religious, and social principles of knighthood during the Middle Ages.

CITADEL Fortress, especially one that guards or dominates a city.

COAT OF ARMS A heraldic design of specific colors and symbols, which a noble family displayed on shields, surcoats, banners, and elsewhere.

CORBEL Projecting block, usually stone, that supports a beam or other horizontal member.

COURTYARD CASTLE Type of castle with a courtyard inside a stone curtain wall. (*see also* CURTAIN WALL)

CRENELLATION Battlements on top of a castle wall, especially those with a series of gaps through which defenders can fire.

CROSSBOW Weapon used to shoot metal bolts using a bow set at right angles to a wooden stock.

CURTAIN WALL Outer wall of a traditional castle.

DRAWBRIDGE Bridge that can be lowered to provide access, and raised to keep out enemies.

DUBBING The act of making a knight, by a blow to the neck or a tap with a sword.

EARTHWORK Fortification consisting of soil mounds, banks, and ditches.

EMBRASURE Beveled or splayed alcove on the inside of an opening in a castle wall, where a gun can be positioned or an archer can load his weapon and shoot.

Bolt

Winch

Bow cord

Giant crossbow called a ballista

FOREBUILDING Structure or building extending out from the front of a great tower; it contains the main entrance and often the chapel. (*see also* GREAT TOWER)

FORT Fortification built to protect defending forces who did not usually live there.

GARDEROBE Lavatory.

GARRISON Company of soldiers who occupy and defend a castle.

GATEHOUSE Large, heavily fortified structure set into the curtain wall of a castle to protect the main entrance. (*see also* CURTAIN WALL)

Gatehouse to Porte St-Michel in the Loire Valley

GAUNTLETS Metal gloves with cuffs, worn as part of a suit of armor.

GREAT TOWER Also called a keep; main tower of a castle, often containing the hall, the lord's private quarters, and store rooms.

HALL Castle's main reception room, used for meals, household and community meetings, and formal occasions. Servants also slept in the hall.

HERALDRY The system of symbolic coats of arms used to identify noble families in battle and elsewhere. (*see also* COAT OF ARMS)

JOUST Competition between two knights, each trying to unhorse the other or shatter each other's lances.

KEEP see GREAT TOWER

Bailey   Motte

Model of a motte-and-bailey castle

KNIGHT Nobly born, highly trained, and fully armored warrior on horseback. (*see also* PAGE, SQUIRE)

LANCE Long, polelike weapon with a wooden shaft and pointed metal head.

LONGBOW Large, powerful wooden bow used to shoot arrows, often over long distances.

LOOPHOLE Narrow opening in a castle wall through which defenders could shoot.

LORD Male knight or noble, often holder of a castle and estate that provide a living for his family, his servants, and the peasants who work his land.

MACE Heavy club with a metal end that sometimes has spikes on it.

MACHICOLATION Projecting structure on top of a castle wall from which defenders could drop missiles on enemies below.

MAIL Protective armor made from small interlinked iron rings.

MANACLES Lockable metal rings used to secure prisoners' hands.

MASTER MASON Skilled craftsman who designed a castle.

MOAT Large, defensive ditch, usually filled with water, that surrounds a castle.

MOTTE Natural or artificial mound on which a castle is built, usually associated with a bailey, as in motte-and-bailey castle. (*see also* BAILEY)

OUBLIETTE Hidden dungeon, often reached through a trap door.

PAGE Young male member of a noble family in the first stage of training for knighthood. (*see also* SQUIRE, KNIGHT)

PALISADE Strong, defensive wooden fence.

PARAPET Low wall on the outer side of a wall-walk. (*see also* WALL-WALK)

PEASANTS People who work on a lord's estate in return for a small plot of land on which they can grow crops to feed themselves and their families.

PLATE ARMOR Suit of armor made up of jointed metal plates.

PORTCULLIS Heavy grille that can be lowered across a castle entrance to keep out enemies.

RIBBED VAULT Framework of diagonally arched ribs supporting a stone ceiling.

SENTRY Soldier who guards a castle and stops strangers from entering.

SIEGE The surrounding and blockading of a castle or other fortified structure in order to capture it.

Mace

SIEGE CAMP Temporary accommodation for attackers undertaking a siege. (*see also* SIEGE)

SIEGE ENGINE Powerful weapon or device (such as a catapult or a battering ram) used to attack a castle. (*see also* SIEGE)

SIEGE TOWER Large covered stairway that can be wheeled up to a castle's walls in order to provide access for attackers. (*see also* SIEGE)

Moat at Herstmonceux Castle, East Sussex, England

SMITH Metal worker. A blacksmith works in iron, a goldsmith in gold, and so on.

SQUIRE Young male member of a noble family who has been a page and moved on to the final stage of training for knighthood. (*see also* PAGE, KNIGHT)

TALUS see BATTER

TOURNAMENT Popular entertainment featuring jousts and mock battles. As well as giving pleasure to the crowds, tournaments provided training for real warfare. (*see also* JOUST, TOURNEY)

TOURNEY Mock battle staged as part of a tournament. (*see also* TOURNAMENT)

TURRET Small tower protruding from a wall and often accommodating a staircase.

UNDERMINING Tunneling under a castle's walls in order to weaken their foundations and bring them down.

VAULT Arched structure that supports a stone ceiling. (*see also* RIBBED VAULT, BARREL VAULT)

VISOR Flap on the front of a helmet that can be pulled down to protect the face.

WALL-WALK Path that runs along the top of a castle wall.

Full set of plate armor

Index

AB

adze, 59
Agincourt, battle of, 10
Alcázar, 16
Alhambra, 17
animals, 54–55
Antioch, 34
aquamanile, 18
aqueduct, 35
armor, 30, 31, 34, 36, 60, 61
armory, 64, 67
arrow loops, 13, 16, 26
Arthur, King, 65
artillery, 24
ashlar, 11
auger, 59,
awl, 59
ax, 53, 59
babies, 46
badges, 31, 37, 44
bailey, 8, 9, 36
bailiff, 66
bakehouse, 40, 43, 67
ballista, 25
barbican, 15, 28
basinet, 30
batter, 28
battering ram, 24
Bayeux Tapestry, 8, 9
Beaumaris, 13
Becket, Thomas, 23
beds, 38
beer, 40, 42
Berry, Duke of, 14, 15, 22
billhook, 59
blockhouse, 18
boar badge, 31
boats, 26
Bodiam, 28
bolts, 26, 27
Bran, 68
bread, 40, 43
brewhouse, 40
bridges, 29
building work, 20, 56–57
burning at stake, 33
butler, 67
buttery, 40

C

Cadbury, 65
Caerleon, 65
Caernarfon, 7, 69
Caerphilly, 12–13, 65
Calais, 27
candlestick, 38

cannon, 36, 62
Canterbury Tales, 46
carpentry, 67
Castel Nuovo, Naples, 28
Castel Sant'Angelo, 69
castellan, 48, 66
catapult, 25
cattle, 54
cauldron, 40
chamberlain, 66
chapel, 21, 22–23
chaplain, 22, 66
Charlemagne, 8
Charles VII, 39
Chateau de
  Chenonceau, 69
Chateau-Gaillard, 64
Chateau d'Ussé, 68
Chaucer, Geoffrey, 46
chemise, 28
chess, 17
chickens, 54
children, 46, 66, 67
Chillon, 32
chisel, 56, 59
clergy, 22–23
coat-of-arms, 14, 31, 38
coat-of-plates, 30, 63
Cochem, 18
concentric castles, 12–13
constable, 66
Constantinople, 35, 62, 64
cooking pot, 20, 40–41
Coucy-le-Chateau, 57
countermining, 24
crags, castle on, 20
crenellation, 13, 16
crenels, 26
Cresci family, 31
criminals, 32
crops, 52–53
crossbows 25, 26, 27
crusades, 34–35, 64
cutlery, 48, 61

DEF

dancing, 45
de Clare, Gilbert, 13
de Male, Louis, 38
de Pisan, Christine, 47
de Vere, Aubrey, 11
Deal 62
dividers, 56
dogs, 67
donjons, 10
Doué-la-Fontaine, 14, 65
drawbridge, 28, 29
drums, 45
dungeons, 32
Edward I, 7, 12, 13
Edward III, 27
Edward IV, 32
Edward V, 32
embrasure, 26

entertainment, 38, 44–45, 67
executioners, 32, 33
Falaise, 6
falconry, 44, 67
fireplaces, 10, 20, 38
flesh-hook, 40
fool, 45, 67
France, 14–15

GH

games, 44, 45
garrison, 30–31, 67
gatehouse, 12, 28
gauntlet, 30
Germany, 18–21
Glamis, 68
goat, 54
Granada, 16, 17
great hall, 38–39, 42
great tower, 10–11
groom, 67
gun ports, 19, 29, 37
guns, 21, 36, 62–63
hall, 38–39, 42
hammer, 59
Hansa bowl, 43
Hastings, 8
Hedingham, 10, 11
Henry II (of England), 23
Henry IV
  (of England), 22
heralds, 24, 67
Himeji, 37
hoarding, 19, 29, 58
Holy Lands, 34–35
horses, 67
horse pendants, 30, 31
horseshoes, 61
houppelande, 66
household, 66–67
Hradcany, 65
hunting, 67
hurdy-gurdy, 45

JK

Japan, 36–37
Jerusalem, 34, 35
jester, 45, 64, 67
jewelry, 47
Joan of Arc, 33
joust, 48, 64
jupon, 30
keep, 10
Kenilworth, 13
Kerak, 34
key, 61
kitchen 40–41, 47, 64, 67
knight, 64, 66, 67
Knights Hospitaller, 35
Knights Templar, 34
Krak des Chevaliers, 35, 64

LM

ladle, 20
lady, 46–47, 66
lady-in-waiting, 67
lamp, 38
lance, 64
Langeais, 29
latrines, 15, 19, 64
laundry, 67
leatherworking, 50
Lichtenstein, 21
lifting bridge, 12
linen, 49, 50
Loches, 22, 23, 33, 39
Loire, 14–15
London, Tower of, 10, 32
longbow, 26
looting, 27
lord, 48–9, 64, 66
Ludwig I
  (of Bavaria), 19, 64
machicolations, 14, 15, 16, 18, 21, 29
Magyars, 65
Maiden Castle, 6
Mallorca, 17
manacles, 32
Marksburg, 20
mason, 7, 10, 56–57, 67
meals, 38–39, 42–3
medallion, 31
merlons, 26
Mespelbrunn, 18
metalwork, 60–61
minstrels, 67
miter, 23
moats, 26, 28, 36
mold, 61
mon, 37
motte and bailey, 8–9
Mowbray family, 31
mummers, 67
murder holes, 28
music, 44–45, 67
Muslims, 16–17, 34–35
Mycenae, 6

NOP

nakers, 45, 67
Naples, 28
Neuschwanstein, 63, 64, 69
Normans, 10
nurse, 67
Orford, 11
Orleans, Duke of, 10
oubliette, 32
ovens, 40
pages, 43, 46, 66, 67
palisade, 6, 26
palliasses, 38

pantry, 40, 67
peasant, 53, 54, 64
Pfalzgrafenstein, 18–19, 29
pheasant, 42
pigs, 54, 55
pincers, 60
pitchfork, 53
planing, 58
plate armor, 30
Pleshey, 7, 9
plowing, 52
plumb line, 57
poetry, 67
portcullis, 12, 18, 28
priest, 66
prison, 10, 14, 32–33, 65
Provins, 10

QR

Qatrana, 35
quiver, 27
quoins, 37
rabbits, 54
Randhausberg, 20
ransom, 32
reeve, 66
Rennes, 9
Restormel, 10
retainer, 67
Rhine, 18
Richard II, 7, 22
Richard III, 32
ringwork, 8, 10
roof, 58
Royal Gold Cup, 22

ST

St. George, 30
Saladin, 34
samurai, 36
San Gimignano, 6
Sanjo Palace, 36
Saumur, 14–15
saw, 59
scaling ladder, 24, 26
seal, 23, 34
Segovia, 16
servants, 66, 67
sheep, 54
sheriff, 48, 66
shield money, 64
shields, 24, 27, 30, 31
shoes, 47
shoguns, 36
sickle, 52
siege castles, 26, 64
siege engines, 12, 24–25
sieges, 17, 24–25, 26, 30, 36
silk, 50
skimmer, 20, 40

smiths, 60–61, 67
snips, 60
soldiers, hired, 67
Sorel, Agnès, 39
sorties, 25, 26
Spain, 16–17
spinning, 51, 66, 67
squires, 43, 46, 64, 66, 67
stable, 67
staircases, spiral, 27
steward, 66
stirrups, 61
storytelling, 44, 67
sugar, 41, 54
surcoat, 34
surrender, 27
table, 38, 42–43
talus, 28, 35
tapestries, 38
Teutonic Order, 18
textiles, 50–51
Thirty Years War, 21
tiles, 14, 20, 38
Tintagel, 65
torture, 32
tournaments, 44, 48, 64
tower, 6, 10, 11
Tower of London, 68, 69
treasurer, 66
trebuchet, 24, 25
trenchers, 43
Très riches heures, 14, 15
Tristan, 15
troubadours, 67
trowel, 56
tunneling, 10, 24

UVWY

Uji River, 36
undermining, 10, 24
underwear, 49, 50
Van, 7
vault, 57
Vikings, 65
vineyards, 15, 52, 53
vintner, 67
wall paintings, 22, 69
warrener, 67
Wasserburg, 18
weaving, 67
well, 15
wheelbarrow, 56
White Tower, 10
Wife of Bath, 46
William the
  Conqueror, 64
wimple, 46
Windsor, 64, 66
women, 30, 46–47, 66
woodworking, 58–59, 67
wool, 50–51
Yelden, 8

Acknowledgments

Dorling Kindersley would like to thank:
the authorities of the following castles and museums for permission to photograph: Caerphilly castle, Dover castle, Hedingham castle, Château de Loches, Marksburg, Pfalzgrafen-stein, Château de Saumur, British Museum, Museum of London; Alex Summers & the Order of the Black Prince for models & objects for photography; the Cotswold Farm Park for animals for photography; Gordon Models for model-making; Joanna Cameron for illustrations; Penny Britchfield, Dorian Davies, Paul Elliott, & Robin Pritchard for acting as models; Nicki Sandford for costumes; Caroline Giles for hair & make-up; Plantagenet Somerset Fry for consultancy; David Ekholm-JAlbum, Sunita Gahir, Susan Reuben, Susan St. Louis, Lisa Stock, & Bulent Yusuf for the clip art; Neville Graham, Sue Nicholson, & Susan St. Louis for the wall chart; Julie Ferrris for proof-reading; Christine Heilman for Americanization.

Picture credits t=top a=above b=below/bottom c=center l=left r=right
Aerofilms: 6bl, 9tl; **Ancient Art & Architecture Collection:** 6cl, 12tl, 32bl, 33tc, 34cr; **Bridgeman Art Library** / British Library: 7rc, 15bl, 22tr, 24tl, 33tr, 39tl, 40tl, 40bl, 431c, 44tr, 44br, 45tl, 46tl, 47bl, 50tc, 52tl, 55tl, 57tl; Bridgeman Art Library, London / New York: British Library, London, UK 66br; / Ecole des Beaux-Arts, Paris: 58bl; London Aerial Photo Library 68tr; Sandro Vannini 69tl; Patrick Ward 68c; Peter Wilson 68bc; **Joe Cornish:** 68-69; **Corbis:** Ric Ergenbright 64cr; Owen Franken 68-69b; Bibliothèque Nationale Paris: 24bl, 35lc, 53tl, 56lc; / University of Oxford for the Bodleian Library: 29cl 451tl, 48c, 54tl; / Musée Conde, Chantilly: 45br; / Giraudon / Musée Conde, Chantilly: 52tr; /

Bibliothèque Municipale de Lyon: 25tr; Laros-Giraudon / Bibliothèque Municipale, Rouen: 50bl; / By Courtesy of the Board of Trustees of the Victoria & Albert Museum: 15tc; /Victoria & Albert Museum, London: 52rc; British Museum: 22cl, 38cl; **English Heritage:** 65tr; **E.T. Archive:** 20tl, 25cl, 27br, 30cr, 31tl, 31bc, 41tl, 481c, 55tr, 60tr, 60br, 62cl, 62tr; **Mary Evans Picture Library:** 18 cr; Flanagans Travels: 71bl; Britstock-IFA: 6tr. Bulloz / Ecole des Beaux-Arts, Paris: 59tc. Jean-Loup Charmet: 20bl; **Werner Forman Archive** / Museum of Catalan Art, Barcelona: 17tl; / Boston Museum of Fine Arts: 37br; / Burke Collection, New York: 36tl; /Kita-In, Saitumi: 36c; **Robert Harding Picture Library:** 8cl, 10lc, 11tc, 28b, 28tl, 29tl, 35t; / British Library: 42tl; / British Museum: 10tr; / Bibliothèque Nationale, Paris: 26tl, 47tl; **Michael Holford:** 8tr, 16-17, 16tl, 36bl;**The Trustees of the Lambeth Palace Library** and his Grace the Archbishop of Canterbury: 32br; **Mark MacLoskey: 6-7; Mansell Collection:** 62tl; **National Maritime Museum:** 70cl; **National**

Portrait Gallery, London: 32cr; **Tony Souter:** 70-71; **Syndication International:** 17tr; / Biblioteca Medicea Laurenziana, Florence: 43tr; / British Museum: 22tl, 52br, 56bc; / Musée du Petit Palais, Paris: 46br; /Trinity College Dublin: 57br; **Wallace Collection:** 67tl 71c; **ZEFA:**17cr,18tr, 20-21, 63tr.

Wall chart credits: The Art Archive: British Museum / Harper Collins Publishers cra.

Jacket images: *Front:* **The Bridgeman Art Library:** British Library tl; **DK Images:** British Museum tr (coin). *Back:* **The Bridgeman Art Library:** British Library bl; **DK Images:** British Museum tl, tr; Museum of London bl (key); Order of the Black Prince cr; Robin Wigington, Arbour Antiques, Ltd., Stratford-upon-Avon fcl

All other images © Dorling Kindersley.
For further information see:
www.dkimages.com